The Book of Good Manners

by W. C. Green

THE BOOK OF GOOD MANNERS is a complete and authentic authority on every single phase of social usage as practiced in America. The author has compiled the matter in dictionary form in order to give the reader the desired information as briefly and clearly as possible, and with the least possible effort in searching through the pages.

ACCEPTING OR DECLINING INVITATIONS. See INVITATIONS, ACCEPTING OR DECLINING.

ACCIDENTS. See STREET ETIQUETTE--MEN--ACCIDENTS.

ADDRESS. The address of a person may be stamped on the stationery.

If the address is stamped, it is not customary to stamp also the crest or monogram.

ADDRESSING ENVELOPES.

MEN. A man should be addressed as Mr. James J, Wilson, or James J. Wilson, Esq. Either the Mr. or the Esq. may be used, but not the two together.

The title belonging to a man should be given. It is not customary to use Mr. or Esq. when Jr. or Sr. is used.

WOMEN. A woman's name should always have the Miss or Mrs.

A woman should never be given her husband's official title, as Mrs. Judge Wilson.

If a woman has a title of her own, she should be addressed as Dr. Minnie Wilson, when the letter is a professional one. If a social letter, this should be Miss Minnie Wilson, or Mrs. Minnie Wilson.

ADDRESSING PERSONS. Young girls should be spoken of as Minnie Wilson, and not as Miss Minnie, but are personally addressed as Miss Minnie. Only the greatest intimacy warrants a man in addressing a young girl as Minnie.

Parents should introduce their daughter as My daughter Minnie, but should speak of them before servants as Miss Minnie.

A married woman should be spoken of as Mrs. Agnes Wilson, and personally addressed as Mrs. Wilson.

ADDRESSING AND SIGNING LETTERS. All answers to invitations should be addressed to the party issuing them.

Letters to a woman who is a comparative stranger may begin My dear Mrs. Wilson, and to a closer acquaintance Dear Mrs. Wilson.

Letters to a man who is a comparative stranger may begin My dear Mr. Wilson, and to a closer acquaintance Dear Mr. Wilson.

For forms of addressing persons with titles, as Mayor, see under that title-- as, Mayor, Governor.

The letters may end, Sincerely yours, or Very truly yours, or I remain yours with kindest regards.

The signature of a man should be John J. Wilson or J. Jones Wilson.

An unmarried woman should sign social letters as Minnie Wilson, and a business letter as Miss Minnie Wilson. A married woman should sign a social letter as Agnes Wilson. In signing a business letter, a married woman may either sign her name Mrs. Agnes Wilson, or, preferably,

Agnes Wilson (Mrs. John Wilson)

AFTERNOON CALLS. These should be made between three and half-past five, and if possible on regular at home days.

In making an afternoon call a man should wear the regulation afternoon dress.

DRESS--MEN. Afternoon dress consists of a double-breasted frock coat of dark material, and waistcoat, either single or double- breasted, of same, or of some fancy material of late design. The trousers should be of light color, avoiding of course extremes in patterns.

White or delicate color linen shirts should be worn, patent leather shoes, silk hat and undressed kid gloves of dark color.

Afternoon dress is worn at weddings, afternoon teas, receptions, garden parties, luncheons, church funerals, and at all afternoon functions.

See also EVENING DRESS--MEN. MORNING DRESS--MEN.

AFTERNOON RECEPTIONS. See AFTERNOON TEAS. GIVEN BY BACHELORS, See BACHELORS' TEAS.

AFTERNOON TEAS (FORMAL). These are very successful as a rule, due perhaps to their small expense and few exactions, and are given with many purposes: to introduce young women into society, to allow a hostess to entertain a number of her friends, to honor some woman of note, etc.

A formal afternoon tea is one for which cards have been issued, naming set date.

Awnings and carpet should be provided from curb to house. A man should be stationed at the curb to open carriage doors and call them when the guests leave, and another African Teas man should be in attendance at the front door to open it the moment a guest appears at the top step and to direct him to the dressing-room.

A policeman should be detailed for the occasion to keep back the onlookers, and should receive a small fee for his services.

At the door of the drawing-room a man should ask the name of each guest, which he announces as the latter enters. The hostess and those receiving with her should be just within the door to receive the guests.

CARDS. Each guest should leave a card in the tray in the hall.

A woman may leave the cards of the men of her family who have been unable to attend.

Cards should be sent by mail or messenger by those invited but unable to be present, and should be timed so that they reach the house during the function.

A husband and wife each send a card when the invitation is issued in the name of the hostess only, and two cards each when issued in the name of hostess and her daughter. If issued in the name of both husband and wife, a husband should send two and his wife should send one card.

DAUGHTERS. The daughters who have passed the debutante age usually stand for an hour beside their mother to receive the guests, and afterward mingle with the guests to help to make the function a success.

DEBUTANTE. When a tea is given in honor of a debutante, she stands beside the hostess (usually her mother), and each guest is introduced to her. Flowers should be liberally provided, and friends may contribute on such an occasion.

The host and the men all wear the regulation afternoon dress.

Women wear costumes appropriate to the afternoon, more elegant in proportion to the elaborateness of the function.

Guests may suit their convenience in arriving, provided they do not come at the opening hour nor at the very end.

After leaving their wraps in the dressing- rooms, guests enter the drawing-room, leaving their cards in the tray in the hall, and then giving their names to the man at the door, who announces them.

On entering the room, the women precede the men.

After greeting the hostess and being introduced to those receiving with her, the guests move into the middle of the room.

Guests go the dining-room when they wish without greeting the hostess.

It is not expected that guests at a large reception will stay all the afternoon. Twenty minutes is long enough. It is not necessary to bid the hostess good-bye when leaving. If guests take leave of host and hostess, they should shake hands.

In the dining-room the men, assisted by the waiters, help the women.

When the reception is a small formal one, the guests may stay a longer time, and usually it is better to take leave of the hostess, unless she is much occupied at the time.

HOST. Except when a newly married couple give a house-warming or a reception, the host does not stand beside his wife, but spends the time in making introductions, and doing his best to make the function a success.

When some married woman or woman guest of honor assists his wife to receive, he should at the proper moment escort her to the dining-room.

HOSTESS. The hostess and those receiving with her should be just within the door, ready to receive each guest as announced.

The hostess shakes hands with each guest, and introduces them to those receiving with her.

Friends assisting a hostess to entertain are generally permitted to invite a few of their own friends, and their cards are sent with those of the hostess. A pretty feature is the presence of a number of young women here and there in the rooms to assist in receiving the guests. Music is always appropriate.

HOURS. The hours are from 4 to 7 P.M.

INTRODUCTIONS. The hostess should introduce her guests to those receiving with her. See also INTRODUCTION.

INVITATIONS. Engraved invitations are sent a week or ten days in advance, by mail or messenger.

They are usually issued in the name of the hostess only, though they may be issued in the name of both husband and wife.

In place of the visiting-card, an "At Home" card may be used, or cards specially engraved for the purpose.

When cards are sent to a married couple, the cards are addressed to both husband and wife.

Invitations are sent in two envelopes-the inner one unsealed and bearing the name of the guest, and the outer one sealed, with, the street address.

INVITATIONS, ANSWERING. It is not necessary to accept or decline these invitations, as the guest accepts by his presence. If unable to do so, he should send by mail or messenger a visiting-card, to reach the hostess during the ceremony.

When the invitation has been issued in the name of the hostess only, a husband and wife each send a card, and if in the name of hostess and her daughter, each should send two cards. If the invitation has been issued in the name of the husband and wife, the wife should send one and a husband two cards.

If the woman in the family is the only one present at the function, she can leave cards for the rest of the family.

MEN. Both the host and men wear the regulation afternoon dress, consisting of the long frock coat with single or double-breasted waistcoat to match, or of some fancy cloth, and gray trousers. White linen, a light tie, a silk hat, gray gloves, and patent leather shoes complete the costume.

The overcoat, hat, and cane are left in the dressing-room, and the guest removes one or both gloves as he pleases--remembering that he must offer his ungloved right hand to the hostess.

SHAKING HANDS. Guests on being presented to the hostess should shake hands. If guest takes leave of hostess, they should shake hands. If the hostess is surrounded by guests, a pleasant nod of farewell is admissible.

WOMEN. Women leave cards of their male relatives as well as their own, even though their names may be announced upon entering. Guests leave their cards in a receptacle provided for the purpose, or give them to the servant at the door.

Women wear a costume appropriate for the afternoon, and keep their hats and gloves on.

AFTERNOON TEAS (INFORMAL). An afternoon tea is a simple entertainment. Refreshments are generally served to the guests. An innovation lately introduced has become quite popular --namely, young women, invited for the purpose, wait upon the guests, bringing in one dainty at a time.

An afternoon tea is called a formal afternoon tea when engraved cards have been issued, naming set date.

CARDS. Guests should leave cards in the hall, or hand them to the servant. Women may leave the cards of the men of her family. Those unable to attend should send card the same afternoon by mail or messenger.

See also AFTERNOON TEAS (Formal)-Cards.

DRESS. Both men and women wear afternoon dress.

GUESTS. All guests, both men and women, wear afternoon dress.

Guests may suit their convenience in arriving or departing--provided they do not come at the opening hour, nor stay to the last moment.

After the guests have left their wraps in the dressing-rooms, they leave their cards in the tray in the hall and enter the drawing- room, the women preceding the men.

After greeting the hostess and being introduced to those assisting her, the guests quietly move away and mingle with the rest.

Each guest goes to the dining-room when he pleases and leaves when he wishes. It is not necessary upon departure to shake hands with the hostess at a large reception, though it is better to do so at a small affair.

It is not necessary for a guest to stay the entire evening; twenty minutes is sufficient.

HOST. If present, he does not receive with his wife. It is not essential that he be present on such an occasion.

HOSTESS. The hostess wears full dress. Daughters may assist, or young women may be asked to do so.

HOURS. From four to seven.

INVITATIONS. For an afternoon tea a visiting- card may be used with the hour and date written or engraved on it. They may be sent by mail or messenger.

The invitation need not be acknowledged.

AFTERNOON WEDDING RECEPTIONS are conducted the same as Wedding Receptions, which see.

AGRICULTURE, SECRETARY OF--HOW ADDRESSED. An official letter begins: Sir, and ends: I have sir, the honor to remain your most obedient servant.

A social letter begins: My dear Mr. Wilson, and ends: I have the honor to remain most sincerely yours.

The address on the envelope is: Hon. John J. Wilson, Secretary of Agriculture.

AISLE PROCESSION. See WEDDING PROCESSION.

ANGLICAN CHURCH ARCHBISHOP. See ARCHBISHOP.

ANGLICAN CHURCH BISHOP. See BISHOP.

ANNIVERSARIES--WEDDING. These are as follows:

First year..................Paper

Fifth year................Wooden

Tenth year ....Tin

Twelfth year.............Leather

Fifteenth year ....Crystal

Twentieth year.............China

Twenty-fifth year.........Silver

Thirtieth year ....Ivory

Fortieth year.............Woolen

Forty-fifth year............Silk

Fiftieth year............ Golden

Seventy-fifth year...... Diamond

Less attention is now paid than formerly to all those before the silver wedding. For specific information, see SILVER WEDDING, TIN WEDDING, etc.

ANNOUNCEMENT--ENGAGEMENT. See ENGAGEMENT PUBLIC ANNOUNCEMENT.

ANNOUNCING GUESTS--BALLS. The hostess decides whether or not the guests are to be announced. At public balls it is customary.

ANSWERING INVITATIONS. See under FUNCTIONS, as DINNERS, INVITATIONS, etc.

APPLES should be pared, cut into small pieces, and eaten with finders or forks.

ARCHBISHOP OF ANGLICAN CHURCH--HOW ADDRESSED. An official letter begins: My Lord Archbishop, may it please your Grace, and ends: I remain, My Lord Archbishop, your Grace's most obedient servant.

A social letter begins: My dear Lord Archbishop, and ends: I have the honor to remain, my dear Lord Archbishop.

The address on the envelop is: The Most Reverend, His Grace the Archbishop of Kent.

ARCHBISHOP OF ROMAN CATHOLIC CHURCH--HOW ADDRESSED. An official or social letter begins: Most Reverend and Dear Sir, and ends: I have the honor to remain your humble servant.

The address on the envelope is: The Most Reverend John J. Wilson, Archbishop of Kent.

ARTICHOKES are eaten with the fingers, taking off leaf by leaf and dipping into the sauce. The solid portion is broken up and eaten with a fork.

ASPARAGUS. The stalks may be taken between the finger and the thumb, if they are not too long, or the green end may be cut off and eaten with a fork, scraping off with the knife what is desired from the remaining part.

AT HOMES.

AFTERNOON AT HOMES. The days for receiving are engraved in the lower left hand corner of the card, with hours specified if one wishes.

No changes should be made in these hours by the hostess unless for exceptional reasons, and she should always be present at the time set.

Unless very intimate, the call should be made only on the specified days.

BACHELORS. It is not customary for a bachelor to use "At Home" cards as a woman does, nor to invite his friends by writing a date and Music at four on his calling-cards in place of an invitation.

DRESS. In the afternoon the caller should wear afternoon dress, and in the evening evening dress.

ACKNOWLEDGING INVITATIONS. Invitations to an ordinary at home need no acknowledgment.

INVITATIONS. Cards for an "At Home" are engraved with the hour for beginning the entertainment--as, Chocolate at 4.30 o'clock. The invitations to a formal "At Home" should be sent in two envelopes, but to an ordinary "At Home" in one envelope. For informal affairs the hour may be written on an ordinary "At Home" card.

BACHELORS' DINNERS. They follow the usual custom of formal dinners, and may be as elaborate as desired. Women may be invited. Such dinners are often given for men only.

CALLS. Women do not call upon a bachelor after attending a dinner given by him.

CHAPERONE. If women are present, a married woman as chaperone is indispensable, and her husband must also be invited. The host should call upon the chaperone and personally request the favor.

The chaperone is taken into dinner by the host, unless the latter takes in the woman in whose honor the dinner may be given. In the latter case, the chaperone is seated at the host's left. She gives the signal for the women to leave the dining-room.

All guests should be introduced to the chaperone, and she should be called upon after a short time by the host.

DRESS. All guests wear evening dress.

HOST. The host should call upon the chaperone within a few days after the dinner.

If men only are present, he either precedes or follows the guests into the dining-room, and if he has given the dinner in honor of some man, he has the latter seated at his right. His duties are the same as the host at dinners.

INVITATIONS. These are usually given in brief notes, but may be engraved, and are similar to the regular invitations to dinners, and are treated accordingly.

MEN. The men wear evening dress, and follow the same etiquette as at other dinners.

WOMEN. The women wear evening dress, and follow the same etiquette as at all dinners, except that no calls are made by them afterward upon the host.

BACHELOR'S FAREWELL DINNER. If the groom wishes, he may give a farewell dinner a few evenings before the wedding to his best man, ushers, and a few intimate friends. He sits at the head of the table and the best man opposite, and on this occasion he may give scarf-pins, link cuff-buttons--or neckties and gloves, if he wishes--to the best man and ushers.

BACHELORS' LUNCHEONS. These are conducted like BACHELOR'S DINNERS, which see. The one difference is that, should the luncheon be given before 6 P.M., afternoon dress should be worn.

BACHELORS' OPERA PARTIES. See THEATRE AND OPERA PARTIES GIVEN BY MEN.

BACHELORS' SUPPERS. These are conducted the same as BACHELOR'S DINNERS, which see.

BACHELORS' TEAS OR AFTERNOON RECEPTIONS.

CHAPERONES. If women are present, a married chaperone is indispensable, who should be the first person invited by personal call.

The chaperone at a small affair pours the tea, and at a large one she receives with the host, and each guest is presented to her.

The host conducts the chaperone to her carriage, and also any other women who may have assisted her.

DRESS. The hosts and guests wear afternoon dress.

INVITATIONS. These maybe oral, brief notes, or, for a large affair, engraved, and should be sent from three days to a week in advance.

HOST. The host should greet his guests at the door, shaking hands with each one, and introducing to the chaperone those not known to her.

He introduces guests who are strangers to each other, bids them adieu, accompanies the women to the door, and escorts the chaperone to her carriage, and if she has come alone without one, may very properly escort her home.

If at a large reception several women have helped him entertain, he should thank them and see them to their carriages.

He will, of course, see that there is provided a dressing-room for women with a maid to wait upon them, and that the rooms are in good order, well furnished with flowers, and that the refreshments are attended to. See also

INVITATIONS.

MEN. Afternoon dress is worn.

WOMEN. The invitations, engraved or oral, should be promptly acknowledged.

Women wear dress customary at afternoon teas, and on their entrance should greet the host. Upon departing they take leave of him, though this is not necessary if the reception be a large one.

If a young woman knows that a chaperone is present, she need not have her own chaperone accompany her.

If the chaperone leaves early, she should do likewise.

BACHELORS' THEATRE PARTY. See THEATRE AND OPERA PARTIES GIVEN BY MEN.

BADGES--BALLS (PUBLIC). It is customary for men and women on the committees to wear on the left side of the breast ornamental badges, embroidered with the official position of the wearer.

BAGGAGE. If a man is traveling with a woman, he should see to the checking and care of her baggage. See also TRAVELING.

WEDDING TRIP. The best man should, some time before the wedding, see that the baggage of the bridal couple has been checked, and the checks given to the groom. See also BEST MAN.

BALLS. A ball is an evening function, beginning at a late hour, devoted wholly to dancing. The costumes are more elaborate, the supper arrangements more extensive, and the floral decorations more lavish than at a dance.

ACCEPTING INVITATION TO DANCE. While a young woman may accept or decline any invitation to dance, it is considered an act of discourtesy to refuse one man for a dance and to accept an invitation thereafter for the same dance from another.

ANNOUNCING GUESTS. The hostess decides whether or not the guests are to be announced. At public balls it is customary.

ANSWERING INVITATIONS. These should be answered immediately, and if declined, the ticket should be returned.

ARRIVING AT. There is no set rule when guests should arrive.

In the city, guests should arrive anywhere between eleven and twelve, and in the country, fifteen minutes after the hour set in the invitation.

ASKING WOMEN TO DANCE. A man asks for the privilege of a dance either with the daughter of the hostess, with any guest of the latter, or with any young woman receiving with her.

On being introduced to a woman, he may ask her for a dance, and should be punctual in keeping the engagement.

It is her privilege to end the dance at any moment she wishes, after which he should conduct her to her chaperone or find a seat for her, after which he is at liberty to go elsewhere.

If for any cause a man has to break his engagements to dance, he should personally explain the matter to every woman with whom he has an engagement and make a suitable apology.

BALLS, ASSEMBLY. The etiquette at an assembly ball is much the same as at a private ball, the functions and duties of the hostess being filled by a committee of women selected for that purpose.

On entering the room, the guests bow to the committee and pass on.

It is not necessary to take leave of the committee.

CARRIAGE. A man should provide a carriage in which to call for the woman he escorts and her chaperone.

CHAPERONES. For a small ball given in a private house, the hostess need not invite the mothers of the young women, and the young women can properly attend, knowing that the hostess will act as a chaperone.

But at a large ball it is necessary to invite the mother as well as the daughters, and the chaperone as well as the debutante under her care. The mother can send regrets for herself, and send her daughters in care of a maid. Or she can attend, and, after remaining a suitable time, she may entrust her daughter to the care of a chaperone who intends to remain the whole evening.

BALLS FOR DEBUTANTE.

DRESS. A debutante should dress in white or some extremely delicate color, and wear very little jewelry--some simple brooch or single piece of jewelry, or a slender chain of pearls.

DUTIES OF DAUGHTERS. Except at her own debut, a daughter does not assist her mother in receiving. She should be ready, however, to see that young women have partners, and to speak, without introduction, to strangers.

GUEST OF HONOR. If the ball is given in honor of some special person, he should be met on his arrival, introduced to the women of the reception committee, escorted to the seat prepared for him, and be looked after the entire evening.

At the end of the ball he should be escorted to his carriage.

DUTIES OF HOST. It is not necessary that a man receive with his wife. He should do all he can to help make the ball successful, especially if his name appears on the invitation. He should assist in finding partners for the women, taking the chaperones into supper, preventing the men from selfishly remaining in the dressing-room, and at the end escorting unattended women to their carriages.

When a formal supper is served, he takes into supper the leading chaperone.

DUTIES OF HOSTESS. As a ball is an entertainment for dancing, it is better to give two small balls where the guests are not crowded than one where they are. It is permissible for a hostess not having sufficient room to hire rooms in some place suitable for the purpose.

In selecting guests, it is wise to have more men present than women.

The hostess should see to it that the rooms are well ventilated and well lighted. An awning and a carpet from the street to the hall door should be provided.

The hostess should stand near the door, prepared to receive the guests as they enter, shaking hands with each one, friend or stranger, and introducing any woman who may receive with her.

A hostess herself should not dance until late in the evening, unless she knows that nearly all her guests have arrived.

A wise hostess will personally see that the women are provided with partners, and that diffident young men are introduced.

The hostess should see that the floor is suitable for dancing, that music is arranged, programs printed, that dressing-rooms, one for the men and one for the women, are arranged for with suitable attendants.

The hostess should stand where the guests can take leave of her, and should shake hands with each when leaving.

HOURS. In the city the hour for a ball to begin is from 10.30 to 11 P.M., but in the country the hour is earlier--from 9 to 9.30.

A public ball begins promptly at the time mentioned in the announcement.

INVITATIONS. These are issued from ten to twenty days before the ball, and should be answered immediately.

For an impromptu dance, they may be issued within a few days of the affair.

These invitations should be engraved. As a general rule, it is not now customary to put on them the letters R. S. V. P.

But when an engraved invitation is posted, two envelopes are used, the inner one bearing the person's name only and unsealed, and the outer bearing both the name and address and sealed.

If the ball has any peculiar feature, as a masquerade or costume, the invitation should have some words to that effect in the lower left hand corner--as, Costume of the XVIIth Century, Bal Masque, or Bal Poudre.

INVITATIONS ASKED FOR STRANGERS. If a hostess receives a request from friends for invitations for friends of theirs, she can properly refuse all such requests, and no friend should feel aggrieved at a refusal for what she has no right to ask and which the hostess is under no obligation to give. If the hostess chooses to grant the request, well and good.

She would naturally do so when the request is for a near relative, or the betrothed of the one making the request.

A man should never ask for an invitation to a ball for another person, except for his fiancee or a near relative.

A woman may ask for an invitation for her fiance, a brother, or a male friend of long standing, or for a visiting friend. She should take care that she does not ask it for some one known to the hostess and whom the latter does not desire to invite. No offense should be felt at a refusal save, possibly, in the case of a brother, sister, or fiance.

INVITATIONS GIVEN BY A NEWCOMER. When a newcomer in a neighborhood desires to give a ball but has no visiting list, it is allowable for her to borrow the visiting list of some friend. The friend, however, arranges that in each envelope is placed a calling-card of her own, so that the invited ones may know that she is acting as sponsor for the newcomer.

INVITATIONS ANSWERED. Every invitation should be answered as soon as possible, and in the third person if the invitation was in the third person. The answer should be sent to the party requesting the pleasure, even if many names are on the invitation.

When a subscriber to a subscription ball invites a friend who is a non-subscriber, she encloses her card in the envelope, and the invited friend sends the answer to the subscriber sending the invitation.

INTRODUCTIONS. When a man is introduced to a woman at a ball, he should ask her for a dance.

MEN AT. Courtesy toward his hostess and consideration for his friends demands that a man who can dance should do so.

To accept an invitation to a ball and then refuse to dance shows that a man is lacking in good breeding.

A man finding few friends at a ball should ask some friend, or the hostess, to introduce him to some women whom he can invite to dance.

It is an act of discourtesy for a man not to request a dance of a woman to whom he has been introduced.

A man escorting a woman to a ball should agree where to meet her after they have each left their wraps at the dressing-rooms. It may be at the foot of the stairway or near the ball-room door.

It is now no longer customary for the man and woman to enter arm in arm, but for the woman to precede the man, and together they greet the hostess. It is for the hostess to merely bow or to shake hands, and the guests follow her lead.

A man should see that his companion's chaperone is comfortably seated, and then ask his companion for a couple of dances, and, with her permission, introduce other young men, who should ask her to dance. Such permission is not usually asked if the man is her fiance, a near relative, or an old friend.

It is strictly the woman's prerogative to decide to retire, and no man should urge or hint to a woman to retire earlier than she wishes.

MEN--CARRIAGE. A man asking a woman to accompany him to a ball should call in a carriage for her and her chaperone.

MEN--DRESS. Men wear full evening dress in summer or winter, city and town.

Gloves of white dressed kid should be worn at all balls.

NEWCOMERS. See BALLS-INVITATIONS GIVEN BY NEWCOMERS.

PATRONESSES. See PUBLIC BALLS--PATRONESSES.

TIPPING SERVANTS. Only at public balls is it customary to give a tip to the men and women in charge of the cloak-room.

SUPPER. Usually a buffet supper, being more easily handled and arranged for. Supper at tables requires many servants, much preparation, and great care.

WOMEN AT. A mother should attend balls with her daughters, going and returning with them, and if she is not invited, they should decline the invitation. The father can act as escort if need be.

After greeting the hostess and guests, the guests pay their respects to the head of the house if he is present.

Taking leave of the hostess is unnecessary.

It is no longer customary for a couple to enter arm in arm, but for the woman to precede the man. A mother, elder sister, or married woman takes the precedence over a daughter, younger sister, or unmarried woman.

If not at once asked to dance, a young woman should take a seat by her chaperone. It is bad taste to refuse a dance with one man and then to dance that same dance with another.

Both the hostess and the women wear their most elaborate costume for such an entertainment- decollete, short-sleeved, and a long train.

For a less elaborate affair the costume may be plainer.

BALLS, ASSEMBLY. See ASSEMBLY BALLS.

BALLS, COSTUME. See COSTUME BALLS.

BALLS, DEBUT. See DEBUT BALLS.

BALLS, PUBLIC. See PUBLIC BALLS.

BALLS, SUBSCRIPTION. See SUBSCRIPTION BALLS.

BANANAS. The skin should be cut off with a knife, peeling from the top down, while holding in the hand. Small pieces should be cut or broken off, and taken in the fingers, or they may be cut up and eaten with a fork.

BARON-HOW ADDRESSED. An official letter begins: My Lord, and ends: I have the honor to be your Lordship's obedient servant.

The address on the envelope is: To the Right Honorable the Baron Wilson.

A social letter begins: Dear Lord Wilson, and ends: Believe me, my dear Lord Wilson, very sincerely yours.

The address is: To the Lord Wilson.

DAUGHTER OF. See DAUGHTER OF BARON.

WIFE OF YOUNGER SON OF. See WIFE OF YOUNGER SON OF BARON.

BARON, YOUNGER SON OF--How Addressed. An official letter begins: Sir, and ends: I have the honor to remain your obedient servant.

A social letter begins: Dear Mr. Wilson, and ends: Believe me, dear Mr. Wilson, sincerely yours.

The address on the envelope is: To the Honorable John Wilson.

BARONESS-HOW ADDRESSED, An official letter begins: Madam, and ends: I have the honor to remain your Ladyship's most obedient servant.

The address on the envelope is: To the Right Honorable The Baroness Kent.

A social letter begins: Dear Lady Kent, and ends. Believe me dear Lady Kent, sincerely yours.

The address is: To the Lady Kent.

BARONET-HOW ADDRESSED. An official letter begins: Sir, and ends: I have the honor to remain, sir, your obedient servant.

A social letter begins: Dear Sir John Wilson, or Dear Sir John, and ends: Believe me, dear Sir John, faithfully yours.

The address on the envelope is: To Sir John Wilson, Bart.

WIFE OF, See WIFE OF BARONET.

BEST MAN. The best man is usually a bachelor, but may be a married man or a widower, and is selected by the groom. He fills an important position, requiring tact, administrative ability, and capacity to handle details. He acts as the groom's representative, confidential advisor, and business advisor.

After his selection he should send a gift to the bride, and may, if he wish, send it to the groom-a custom not yet clearly established, and one not to be either encouraged or followed with safety.

On the morning of the wedding-day he should have received both the ring and fee from the groom, and should personally see to the church and other details.

He breakfasts with the groom, and together they drive to the church.

CALLS. He should call on the bride's mother within two weeks after the ceremony, and also on the married couple upon their return from their wedding trip.

CHURCH. He accompanies the groom into the chancel, and stands by his side till the bride appears, when he receives the groom's hat and gloves, and stands a little way behind him. When the clergyman bids the bride and groom join hands, he gives the ring to to the groom.

At the conclusion of the ceremony, he gives the wedding fee to the clergyman, and hastily leaves the church to summon the groom's carriage and to return him his hat. He signs the register, if a witness is needed.

It is a better arrangement to have the groom and the best man enter the church without their hats, and have the latter sent from the vestry to the church door, so that the groom may receive his when he leaves the church.

Especially is this a good arrangement if the best man has to walk with the maid of honor down the aisle.

After this, he hastens in his own carriage to the bride's home, to assist in meeting and introducing the guests at the reception or breakfast.

DRESS. If the bride presents the best man with the boutonniere, he should go to her house on the wedding-day to have her put it in the lapel of his coat.

He should dress as nearly as possible like the groom-wearing afternoon dress at an afternoon wedding, and at an evening wedding evening dress.

See also GROOM-DRESS.

EXPENSES. The best man is the guest of the groom, and in matters of expense this should be borne in mind.

REPORTERS. If such is the wish of the family of the bride, the best man attends to the reporters, and furnishes them with the names of groom, bride, relatives, friends, description of gowns, and other details deemed suitable for publication.

WEDDING BREAKFAST. The best man escorts the maid of honor, and they are usually seated at the bridal table.

WEDDING RECEPTION. The best man stands with the married couple, and is introduced to the guests.

WEDDING TRIP. He should arrange beforehand all details of the trip-as to tickets, parlor-car, flowers, baggage, etc. He alone knows the point of destination, and is in honor bound not to betray it, save in case of emergencies. He should see that the married couple leave the house without any trouble, and if the station is near, he should go in a separate carriage (provided by the groom) to personally attend to all details. He is the last one to see the married couple, and should return to the house to give their last message to the parents.

BEST WISHES TO BRIDE. One should give best wishes to the bride and congratulations to the groom.

BICYCLING. A man bicycling with a woman should extend to her all the courtesies practised when riding or driving with her, such as allowing her to set the pace, taking the lead on unfamiliar roads and in dangerous places, riding on the side nearest obstacles, etc.

MEN--DRESS. A man should wear the regulation suit coat, waistcoat, and knickerbockers of gray or brown tweed, avoiding all eccentricities of personal taste.

BIRTH (Announcement). If wishing to send congratulations after a birth, cards should be left in person or sent by a messenger. Cut flowers may be sent with the card.

BISHOP OF THE ANGLICAN CHURCH--HOW ADDRESSED. An official letter begins: My Lord, and ends: I have the honor to remain your Lordship's most obedient servant.

A social letter begins: My Dear Lord Bishop, and ends: I have the honor to remain, my Dear Lord Bishop, faithfully yours.

The address on the envelope: To the Right Rev. The Lord Bishop of Kent.

BISHOP (PROTESTANT)-HOW ADDRESSED. An official letter begins: Right Reverend and Dear Sir, and ends: I have the honor to remain your obedient servant.

A social letter begins: Dear Bishop Wilson, and ends: I remain sincerely yours.

The address on the envelope is: To the Right Reverend John J. Wilson, Bishop of, Montana.

BISHOP (ROMAN CATHOLIC)--HOW ADDRESSED. An official or social letter begins. Right Reverend and Dear Sir, and ends: I have the honor to remain your humble servant.

The address on the envelope is: To the Right Reverend John J. Wilson, Bishop of Ohio.

BONNETS (THEATRE). A woman of any consideration should either wear no bonnet or remove it when the curtain rises.

It would be in place for a man or a woman to politely request a woman whose bonnet obstructs the view to remove it, and, after it was done, to thank the woman for so doing.

BOUQUETS (WEDDING). The bouquet carried by the bride is furnished by the groom, who should also provide bouquets for the bridesmaids.

BOWING

MEN, When leaving a woman at the door of her house, he bows and retires as the door is opened.

When seeing a woman to her carriage, he should raise his hat on closing the door.

On a railroad a man removes his hat in a parlor-car, but not in a day coach.

In street-cars a man should raise his hat when giving his seat to a woman; also when rendering a service to a woman in public, in answering a question, or in apologizing to a woman.

In elevators, when women are present, the hat should be removed.

In hotel halls or corridors a man passing a woman should raise his hat.

Men do not raise their hats to one another, save out of deference to an elderly person, a person of note, or a clergyman.

In driving, if impossible to raise the hat, he should touch it with his whip.

The hat is gracefully lifted from the head, brought to the level of the chest, and the body inclined forward, and then replaced in passing.

It is the woman's privilege to bow first if it is a mere acquaintance. If, however, a woman bows, and the man fails to recognize her, he should bow in return.

A man may bow first to a very intimate friend.

Meeting a woman to whom he has been introduced at an entertainment, he should wait until she bows first.

After bowing to a woman, the man may join her, and with her permission may walk a short distance with her.

He should not stand in the street and converse with her any length of time. She may excuse herself and pass on. He should not feel affronted.

If he meets a woman he does not know accompanied by a man he does know, both men bow.

The man accompanying her should bow to every man or woman to whom she bows.

WOMEN. A woman's bow should be dignified-- a faint smile and a gentle inclination of the head.

Women bow first to men when meeting in the street. A man may bow first if the acquaintance is intimate.

When walking with a man, and they meet another unknown to her, but known to her escort, both men bow. If she meets a friend, man or woman, unknown to her escort, he bows.

Unless an introduction has taken place at any function, no recognition is customary. It is the woman's privilege, however, to decide for herself whether she will recognize the guest or not.

A man bowing and joining a woman on the street must ask permission to do so. She is at perfect liberty to gracefully decline.

If a man stops to talk on the street, she may excuse herself and pass on. If she continues the conversation and he stands with his hat in his hand, she may request him to replace it. Such conversations should be brief.

BREAD should be broken into small pieces, buttered, and transferred with the fingers to the mouth. The bread should be placed on the small plate provided for the purpose.

BREAKFASTS. Breakfasts are generally given from ten to twelve in the morning. Very formal breakfasts are held at twelve o'clock.

CALLS. A call need not be made after a simple breakfast, but obligatory after a formal one.

DRESS. Street costumes are worn by men and women.

GUESTS. Guests leave half an hour after the breakfast.

HOURS. The hour is from 12 to 12.30.

INVITATIONS. Cards are engraved and sent a week in advance for formal breakfasts, but for informal breakfasts they may be written. If given in honor of a special guest, the name is engraved on the card--as, TO MEET MR. WILSON.

MEN. Men are usually invited, and they are often given for men. Men wear street costume.

Guests should leave half an hour after breakfast. A call is not necessary after a simple breakfast, but obligatory after a formal one.

MEN LEAVING CARDS. After a breakfast a man should leave a card for host and hostess, whether the invitation was accepted or not. Or it may be sent by mail or messenger, with an apology for so doing.

WOMEN. Women wear street costume, including gloves, the latter being taken off at table. Women remove their coats and wraps, but not bonnets.

Guests should leave half an hour after breakfast. A call is not necessary after a simple breakfast, but obligatory after a formal one.

WEDDING. See WEDDING RECEPTIONS OR BREAKFASTS.

BREAKING DINNER ENGAGEMENTS. When it is absolutely necessary to break an engagement made for a dinner, a letter should be sent as soon as possible to the hostess, either by special delivery or messenger, giving the reason and expressing regrets.

BRIDE. The bride selects the church and the clergyman, and can, if she wishes, ask the latter personally or by note to perform the ceremony. She selects the music for the ceremony and the organist, names the wedding day, and selects the ushers and the bridesmaids. Of the bridesmaids, she may select one, some near friend, as the maid of honor, to act for her, as the best man does for the groom.

She further designates one of the ushers to be master of ceremonies, and should instruct him minutely as to the details she desires carried out-how the wedding party shall enter the church, proceed up the aisle, etc.

A few days before the wedding she gives a dinner to the bridesmaids and maid of honor, who take this opportunity to examine the trousseau. The ushers, best man, and groom may come after the dinner to attend the wedding rehearsal. These rehearsals should be gone through carefully, and if they can be held at the church so much the better. Each person should be instructed by note as to their duties, as this prevents confusion.

CHURCH. On the wedding-day, after receiving the bridesmaids and maid of honor at her house, she goes to the church with her father (or nearest male relative), and leans upon his arm as they proceed up the aisle, following the bridesmaids, and carrying her bridal bouquet (or, if she wishes, a prayer-book).

Arriving at the chancel, she leaves her father and steps forward to take the left arm of the groom, who advances from the chancel to meet her. They stand before the clergyman, and, if they wish, may kneel, and upon rising stand about a foot apart.

At the words of the ceremony, "Who giveth this woman away?" or, "To be married to this man?" her father advances and places her right hand in that of the clergyman, who places it in the groom's right hand. After this her father retires to his seat in the pew with his family.

When the plighting of the troth comes, the groom receives the ring from the best man and hands it to the bride, who gives it to the clergyman. He returns it to the groom, who then places it on the third finger of the bride's left hand. When plighting the troth, the bride gives her glove and bouquet to the maid of honor, or, what is better, the finger of the glove may be cut to allow the ring to be placed on without the glove being removed.

The kiss at the altar is no longer in good form.

At the end of the ceremony, after the clergyman has congratulated the married couple, the bride takes her husband's right arm and they lead the procession to the vestibule, where they receive the congratulations of near friends. Here the maid of honor and bridesmaids cloak and prepare the bride for the trip home in the groom's carriage.

DRESS. The bride is veiled, and is dressed in white-full dress, day or evening. Gloves need not be worn in the church. The bridesmaids provide their own outfit, unless the bride asks them to dress in a style of her own selecting. In this case, she supplies them gowns, hats, gloves, and shoes, as she may wish.

FAREWELL LUNCHEON. While a farewell luncheon given to the bridesmaids by the bride is not necessary, yet it is a pleasant way for a woman to entertain her female friends the last time in her father's house.

On this occasion it is a good plan for the bride to give to the maid of honor and brides-maids her souvenirs, which, of course, should be alike, and of use at the wedding ceremony.

GIFTS. The bride may give to the groom a ring as an engagement ring if she wishes. She should make suitable gifts to the bridesmaids as souvenirs of the occasion, and may also present them with flowers. If she presents boutonnieres to the best man and the ushers, they should appear at her house before the ceremony and have her place them in the lapel of their coats.

She should acknowledge immediately the receipt of all wedding gifts.

GLOVES. The bride need not wear gloves in the church.

INVITATIONS. At a church wedding the bride usually provides the bridesmaids with extra invitations for their personal use.

KISS. Only the parents of the bride and her most intimate relatives should kiss the bride. It is now no longer good form for all to do so.

SEEING GROOM ON WEDDING-DAY. It is not customary for the bride to see the groom on the wedding-day till she meets him at the altar.

WEDDING BREAKFAST. The bride and groom occupy the centre one of the small tables.

At all wedding breakfasts it is customary for the guests to assemble in the drawing-room, and then to enter the breakfast-room together--the bride and groom leading the way.

It is not usual to have the bridal cake at a wedding breakfast, but if such is the case, the bride makes the first cut, and the slices are given first to those at the bridal table.

WEDDING RECEPTION. She should stand by her husband's side to receive the best wishes of all present. The guests are not announced, but are introduced by the ushers to the bride if not known to her.

The bride should not leave her place to mingle with the guests until all have been introduced to her.

BRIDE'S FAMILY. See FAMILY OF BRIDE.

BRIDE'S FATHER. See FATHER OF BRIDE.

BRIDE'S MOTHER. See MOTHER OF BRIDE.

BRIDEGROOM. See GROOM.

BRIDESMAIDS. The bridesmaids are selected by the bride, and number six, eight, or twelve-- mostly eight. She usually gives them a dinner a few days before the wedding, at which she shows them the trousseau and discusses the details of the wedding.

The ushers and the groom are invited to come after the dinner, and then the rehearsal takes place. The bridesmaids should be present at this and all other rehearsals, and if unable to be present at the wedding should give the bride ample notice, that a substitute may be secured.

CALLS. They call upon the mother of the bride within a week or ten days after the ceremony, and upon the bride, in her own home, after her return from her wedding trip.

CARRIAGES. A carriage provided by the family of the bride calls for the bridesmaid on the wedding-day, and takes her to the bride's house. Her carriage follows the bride's to the church, and, after the ceremony, takes her to the wedding breakfast or reception.

CHURCH. They meet at the house of the bride, and there take their carriages to the church. While their carriages follow that of the bride, they alight first and receive her in the vestibule. They may carry bouquets supplied by the bride's family or the groom.

In the procession tip the aisle they follow the ushers, walking two by two, and as the ushers approach the altar they divide--one-half to the right and one-half to the left. The bridesmaids do likewise, leaving space for the bridal party to pass.

In the procession down the aisle they follow the best man and maid of honor to the vestibule, where, after giving their best wishes to the bride, and congratulations to the groom, they return to the bride's home to assist in entertaining the guests at the reception or breakfast.

DANCING. At the wedding breakfast or reception dancing is sometimes indulged in.

DINNER TO MARRIED COUPLE. The bridesmaids usually give a dinner to the married couple on the latter's return from their wedding trip.

DRESS. They usually follow the wishes of the bride in the matter of dress. Should she desire any particular style of dress, entailing considerable expense, on account of novelty or oddity, she usually presents them the outfit, which it is permissible for them to accept.

If the bride has no particular wish, they decide the matter among themselves, always bearing in mind that their style of dress and material must be subordinated to that of the bride, and that there could be no greater exhibition of lack of refinement and good taste than for any bridesmaid to make herself in any way more attractive than the bride.

GIFTS. It is customary for them to send a wedding gift to the bride.

They usually receive a pretty souvenir from the bride and a bouquet from the groom.

INVITATIONS. At a large church wedding several invitations are usually given to the bridesmaids for their own personal use.

REHEARSALS. They should be present at all rehearsals.

WEDDING BREAKFASTS. They pair off with the ushers, and are usually seated at a table by themselves.

WEDDING RECEPTIONS. They stand beside the married couple, and are introduced to the guests.

BROTHER AT DEBUT. A brother, when his sister's debut takes the form of a supper or dinner, should take his sister (the debutante) into dinner or supper.

BUTLER--TIPS. It is customary for a man leaving a house-party where he has been a guest to tip the butler who acted as a valet.

CABINET (U. S,), MEMBER OF--HOW ADDRESSED. An official letter begins: Sir, and ends: I have, sir, the honor to remain your most obedient servant.

A social letter begins: My dear Mr. Wilson, and ends: I have the honor to remain most sincerely yours.

The address on the envelope is: Hon. John J. Wilson, Secretary of State.

CAKE. is broken into pieces, the size of a mouthful, and then eaten with fingers or fork.

CALLS. Unless close intimacy exists, calls should only be made on the specified days.

ASKING MEN TO CALL ON WOMEN. A debutante should leave this matter to her mother or chaperone.

A young woman, until she has had some experience in society, should be very careful in inviting men to call.

She should not invite a man to call whom she has met for the first time. No man should be invited to call until she is assured of his social standing and character.

In some parts of the country men first ask permission to call, and in other parts women first ask men to call.

ASKING WOMEN TO CALL ON WOMEN. It is generally the custom for the married or elder woman to ask the unmarried or younger woman to call.

BACHELORS' DINNERS. See BACHELORS' DINNERS --CALLS.

BREAKFAST. See BREAKFASTS--CALLS.

BEST MAN. See BEST MAN--CALLS

BRIDESMAIDS. See BRIDESMAIDS--CALLS.

CHAPERONES. See CHAPERONES--MEN CALLING.

BUSINESS. A business man may call in street dress upon a woman before six o'clock.

Social visits may be made in the same manner.

DAYS AT HOME. Calls should only be made on the regular "At Home" days, and the hostess should always be present on that day. Very intimate friends may set aside this rule.

DEBUTANTE. See DEBUTANTE--CALLS.

DRESS. When making an afternoon call, a man would wear afternoon dress, and evening dress in making an evening call.

HIGH TEA. See HIGH TEA--CALLS.

HOURS. When no special day for receiving is indicated, calls may be made at any proper hour, according to the custom of the locality. Men of leisure may call at the fashionable hours from two till five in the afternoon, while business and professional men may call between eight and nine in the evening, as their obligations prevent them from observing the fashionable hours.

LENGTH. A formal call may last from fifteen to thirty minutes. Old friends may stay longer.

LUNCHEONS. See LUNCHEON--CALLS.

MEN. AFTER ENTERTAINMENTS. After an entertainment a man should call in person on host and hostess, whether the invitation was accepted or not. If a card is sent or mailed, it should be accompanied with an apology.

To call on an acquaintance in an opera box does not relieve one of the duty of making a formal call in return for social favors.

When calling on the hostess but not on the host, a man should leave a card for him. If the hostess be out, he should leave two cards.

Married men can return their social obligations to women by personal calls, or the women of the family can leave the men's cards with their own.

A call should be made the day following a luncheon or a breakfast; the same after a dinner, or at least within a week. A call should be made within a week after a ball.

After a theatre party given by a man, he should call within three days on the woman he escorted, or leave his card, and should call within a week on the remainder of his guests.

MEN CALLING ON MEN. At the beginning of the season it is usual to leave a card for each member of a family called on--one card for husband, wife, "misses," and guest, or rest of the family. Sometimes two cards answer the purpose.

They may be sent by mail or messenger.

MEN CALLING ON WOMEN. A man should call only on "At Home" days, especially when making the first call, unless specially invited. He should call at the hour appointed.

When no special day for receiving is indicated, calls may be made at any proper hour, according to the custom of the locality. Men of leisure may call at the fashionable hours --from two till five o'clock.

Business and professional men may call between eight and nine o'clock, as their obligations prevent them from observing the fashionable hours.

A business man may call in street dress before six o'clock, and the same dress in the evening, if intimately acquainted.

Informal calls may be made on Sunday after three o'clock by business and professional men, provided there are no religious or other scruples on the part of those receiving the calls.

Evening or other than mere formal calls should not be made, save by special invitation.

The first call should last not longer than ten or fifteen minutes. It is correct to ask for all the women of the family.

At the first call he should give his card at the door. At following calls it is optional whether to give a card or merely the name, asking at the same time for the person one desires to see. When the servant's intelligence seems doubtful, or the name is an unusual one, it is safer to give a card.

When a woman invites a man to call without specifying when, it is not considered as an invitation at all, but merely as a formal courtesy.

It is bad form to solicit by innuendo or otherwise an invitation to call from a woman. It is her privilege to make the first move in such matters; otherwise she would be placed in an embarrassing position.

When an invitation specifies the hour, every effort should be made to be punctual. It is impolite to be too early or too late.

At a formal call, when others are present, a man should not be seated unless invited to do so. He should leave as others come in, and not remain longer than ten or fifteen minutes.

A man having a card or letter of introduction to a young woman should present it in person to the chaperone. If she is out, he should mail it to her, and she should at once notify him whether he may call.

If a caller is a stranger to the young woman's hostess, he should send his card to the latter and ask to see her.

The chaperone may, if desirable, give a man permission to call upon the woman under her charge.

A man should not call upon an unmarried woman until invited by her to do so. He may ask a married woman who has a family for permission to call.

GLOVES. Gloves need not be removed at a formal or brief call.

ENTERTAINMENTS. At entertainments a man should give his card to the servant at the door or leave it in the hall.

A few appropriate words of greeting should be addressed to the hostess and host as soon after entering as possible.

Personal introductions are not absolutely required at musicales, teas, "At Homes," etc. One may converse with those nearest, but this does not warrant future recognition.

When light repasts are served, as teas, ices, etc, a man should put his napkin on his knee and hold the plate in his hand.

He should depart with as little ceremony as possible--a bow and a smile, if host and hostess are engaged, are sufficient. He should not shake hands and try to speak unless it can be done without becoming conspicuous.

MEN CALLING ON WOMEN--HAT. A man making a formal or brief call should carry his hat in his hand into the parlor.

SHAKING HANDS. A man should not offer to shake hands first, as that is the privilege of the women.

MEN--DRESS. In making ceremonious calls, men wear afternoon dress, and after six o'clock evening dress.

See also AFTERNOON DRESS--MEN. EVENING DRESS--MEN.

PALL-BEARERS. See PALL-BEARERS--CALLS.

THEATRE. See THEATRE--CALLS.

USHERS. See USHERS--CALLS.

WEDDING INVITATIONS. Very intimate friends can call personally. Friends of the groom who have no acquaintance with the bride's family should send their cards to those inviting them.

Those who do not receive wedding invitations, announcement, or "At Home" cards should not call on the married couple, but consider themselves as dropped from their circle of acquaintance.

WOMEN RECEIVING AND INVITING MEN. The invitation to call should be extended by the woman, and if she does not specify the time, will naturally be considered as an act of courtesy, but not as an invitation.

These invitations should be given with great care by young women. It is better to have the invitation extended by her mother or chaperone.

A married woman may ask a man to call, especially if she have unmarried daughters. An afternoon tea is an appropriate time to specify. A man may ask a married woman who has a family for permission to call.

At the beginning of a season, a man who desires the further acquaintance of a woman should leave his card in person for all the members of the family.

A formal call, or the first call of the season, should, mot last longer than ten or fifteen minutes. It is proper for the man to inquire for all the women of the family.

A man should call only on "At Home" days, unless especially invited to come at other times. The hostess should be home on all "At Home" days, unless sickness or other good cause prevents.

In the absence of "At Home" days, or specified time, calls may be received at any proper hour, according to the locality of the place.

When men make a formal call at other than specified time, the hostess may justly excuse herself. The caller would have no ground for offense.

Intimate friends need not hold to formal hours for paying calls.

Men of leisure should call only at fashionable hours--from two to five in the afternoon.

Evening calls should not be made by other than business or professional men, unless the acquaintance be an intimate one, or unless they are specially invited.

Business and professional men may call between eight and nine o'clock, as their obligations prevent them from observing the fashionable hours.

Informal calls may be made on Sunday after three o'clock by business and professional men, provided there are no religious or other scruples on the part of those receiving the calls.

A business man may call in street dress before six o'clock in the evening, or thereafter if intimacy warrants.

Evening, or other than mere formal calls, should not be made, save by special invitation.

A man should leave his card when calling. If his hostess is married, he should leave one also for the host. If she is out, he should leave two.

When calling upon a young woman whose hostess is not known to the man, he should send his card to her.

If the woman is seated when a man enters the room, she rises to greet him, and, if she wishes, shakes hands. It is her option to shake hands or not, and she should make the first advances. It is bad form for him to do so.

During a formal call, when other guests are present, a man should remain standing and depart upon the entrance of others. If the hostess is seated at the time, she need not rise or shake hands, but merely bow.

The hostess should not accompany a caller to the door of the parlor, but bow from her chair.

Dropping in at a theatre or opera party does not relieve a man from making formal calls that may be due.

A woman's escort to a theatre party should call upon her within a week. If she were his guest, he should do so within three days, or send his card, with an apology.

Business calls are privileged, and can be made when convenient, although preferably by appointment.

WOMEN RECEIVING--INTRODUCTIONS. At formal calls conversation should be general among the guests. Introductions are unnecessary.

AFTERNOON. See AFTERNOON CALLS.

COUNTRY. See COUNTRY CALLS.

EVENING. See EVENING CALLS.

FIRST. See FIRST CALLS.

INVALID'S. See INVALID'S CALLS.

SUNDAY. See SUNDAY CALLS.

CANCELING DINNERS. When it becomes necessary for a hostess to cancel or postpone a dinner, she should send as soon as possible, either by special delivery or messenger, a letter to each guest who has accepted the invitation. The letter, written either in the first or third person, should state the reason and express regrets.

CANCELING WEDDINGS. See WEDDINGS-INVITATIONS RECALLED.

CANES. A cane is the correct thing for a man when walking, except when engaged in business. It should be held a few inches below the knob, ferrule down, and should, like umbrellas, be carried vertically.

CALLING. When making a formal or brief call the cane should be left in the hall.

CARDINAL-HOW ADDRESSED. A letter, official or social, begins: Your Eminence, and ends: I have the honor to remain your humble servant. The address on the envelope is: His Eminence Cardinal Wilson.

CARDS.

DEBUT. See DEBUT CARDS.

DEBUTANTS. See DEBUTANTE CARDS.

INFANT. See INFANT'S CARDS.

IN MEMORIAM. See IN MEMORIAM CARDS.

MOURNING. See MOURNING CARDS.

CARDS, VISITING.

ADDRESSING. See ADDRESSING CARDS (VISITING).

AFTERNOON TEAS. See CARDS (VISITING), LEAVING IN PERSON--AFTERNOON TEAS. CARDS (VISITING), MAIL OR MESSENGER-AFTERNOON TEAS.

AT HOME. See AT HOME-CARDS.

BIRTH (ANNOUNCEMENT). See CARDS (VISITING), LEAVING IN PERSON--BIRTH.

CONDOLENCE. See CONDOLENCE--CARDS.

DAUGHTER. See DAUGHTERS--CARDS (VISITING).

GARDEN PARTIES. See GARDEN PARTIES--CARDS.

HUSBAND AND WIFE. When the wife is calling, she can leave cards of the husband and sons if it is impossible for them to do so themselves.

After an entertainment, cards of the family can be left for the host and hostess by either the wife or any of the daughters. See Also MR. AND MRS. CARD.

LEAVING IN PERSON. When cards with a message of congratulation are left in person, nothing should be written on it.

LEAVING IN PERSON--AFTERNOON TEAS. Women leave cards of their male relatives as well as their own, although their names may be announced upon entering the drawing-room. Guests leave their cards in a receptacle provided, or give them to the servant at the door.

MEN. A bachelor should not use AT HOME cards as a woman does, nor to invite his friends by writing a date and MUSIC AT FOUR on his calling card in place of an invitation.

MEN--LEAVING IN PERSON. When returning to town after a long absence, a man should leave cards having his address.

When calling upon a young woman whose hostess is not known by the man, he should send his card to her.

At the beginning of a season, a man should leave two cards for all those whose entertainments he is in the habit of attending, or on whom he pays social calls. These cards may also be mailed. If left in person, there should be one for each member of the family called upon, or only two cards. In the former there should be left one card for the host, one for the hostess, one for the "misses," and one for the rest of the family and their guest.

Men of leisure should leave their own cards, while business men can have them left by the women of the family.

The corner of the card should not be turned down.

Cards are now left in the hall by the servant and the caller is announced. In business calls the card is taken to the person for whom the caller asked.

When calling, a man should leave a card whether the hostess is at home or not.

P. P. C. card's may be left in person or sent by mail upon departure from city, or on leaving winter or summer resort.

When a man calls upon a young woman whom a hostess is entertaining, he should leave cards for both.

When a man calls upon another man, if he is not at home, he should leave a card.

When a man calls on the hostess but not the host he should leave a card for him. If the hostess is out, he should leave two cards--one for each.

BREAKFASTS, LUNCHEONS, DINNERS. A man should leave a card the day after a breakfast, luncheon, or dinner for the host and hostess, whether the invitation was accepted or not. They may also be sent by mail or messenger, with an apology for so doing.

BALLS, SUBSCRIPTION. Shortly after receiving an invitation to a subscription ball, a man should leave a card for the patroness inviting him.

DEBUTANTE. When calling upon a debutante a man should leave cards for her mother, whether the entertainment was attended or not.

ENTERTAINMENT BY MEN. After a man's formal entertainment for men, a man should leave a card within one week, whether the event was attended or not. It can be sent by mail or messenger.

RECEPTION. When the host and hostess receive together, a man should leave one card for both, and if not present at the reception, he should send two cards.

THEATRE. After a theatre party given by a man, he should call within three days on the woman he escorted or leave his card.

WEDDING RECEPTION. After a wedding reception a man should leave a card for the host and hostess, and another for the bridal couple.

If a man has been invited to the church but not to the wedding reception, he should leave a card for the bride's parents and the bridal couple, or should mail a card.

SENDING BY MAIL, OR MESSENGER. After an entertainment a man should call in person on host and hostess, whether the invitation was accepted or not. If a card is mailed or sent, it should be accompanied with an apology.

At the beginning of the season a man should leave cards for all those whose entertainments he is in the habit of attending, or on whom he pays social calls. These cards may also be mailed. If left in person, there should be one for each member of the household or only two cards.

In the former case, there should be left one card for the host, one for the hostess, one for the "misses," and one for the rest of the family and the guest.

If a man is unable to make a formal call upon a debutante and her mother at her debut, he should send his card by mail or messenger.

A man may mail his card to a woman engaged to be married, if acquaintance warrants.

Visitors to town should send cards to every one whom they desire to see. The address should be written on them.

AFTERNOON TEA. If a man is unable to be present at an afternoon tea, he should send a card the same afternoon.

BREAKFASTS, LUNCHEONS, DINNERS. A man should leave a card the day after a breakfast, luncheon, or dinner for the host and hostess, whether the invitation was accepted or not. They may be sent by mail or messenger with an apology for so doing.

ENTERTAINMENT BY MEN. After a man's formal entertainment for men, a man should leave a card within one week, whether the event was attended or not. It can be sent by mail or messenger.

P. P. C. cards may be sent by mail or messenger upon departure from city, or on leaving winter or summer resort.

RECEPTION. When the host and hostess receive together, a man should leave one card for both, and, if not present at the reception, he should send two cards.

WEDDING RECEPTION. If a man has been invited to the church but not the wedding reception, he should leave or mail a card to the bride's parents, and also to the bridal couple.

STYLE. The full name should be used, and if too long, the initials only. The club address is put in the lower left-hand corner, and if not living at a club, the home address should be in lower right-hand corner. In the absence of a title, Mr. is always used on an engraved but not a written card.

Cards should be engraved in plain letter, according to prevailing fashion.

Facsimile cards engraved are no longer used.

Written cards are in bad taste, but in case of necessity they may be used. The name should be written in full if not too long, and should be the autograph of the sender.

Messages or writing should not appear on men's cards. If address is changed, new cards should be engraved. In an emergency only the new address may be written.

MOURNING CARDS are the same size as visiting- cards, and a black border is used--the width to be regulated by the relationship of the deceased relative.

MEN--STYLE, TITLES. Men having titles use them before their names--as, Reverend, Rev., Mr., Dr., Army and Navy titles, and officers on retired list.

L.L.D. and all professional titles are placed after the name. Political and judicial titles are always omitted.

Physicians may use Dr. before or M.D. after the name. On cards intended for social use, office hours and other professional matter are ommitted.

MR. AND MRS. See MR. AND MRS. CARDS.

P. P. C. See P. P. C. CARDS.

SENDING BY MAIL OR MESSENGER. If after accepting an invitation it is necessary to decline, a card should be sent the evening of the entertainment, with an explanatory note the day following.

When an invitation has been received to an "At Home" debut, and one has not been able to attend, cards should be sent by mail or messenger, to arrive at the time of the ceremony.

A card should be mailed to a man engaged to be married.

AFTERNOON TEAS. The invitations to a formal afternoon tea are sent a week or ten days in advance by mail or messenger. No reply is necessary, but if unable to be present, a card should be sent the day of the entertainment.

For an afternoon tea a visiting-card may be used, with the hour for the "tea" written or engraved over the date beneath the fixed day of that week. They may be sent by mail or messenger.

Persons unable to attend should send cards the same afternoon.

BIRTH (ANNOUNCEMENT). If wishing to congratulate after a birth, cards should be left in person or sent by a messenger. Cut flowers may be sent with the card.

CONDOLENCE. After a death in the family of an acquaintance, a card with the word Condolence written on it should be left in person or by messenger. For very intimate acquaintances, cut flowers may be left in person or sent, together with a card or letter.

When unable to leave in person a card with Condolence written on it, send it to intimate friends only with a note of apology. If out of town, it should be sent with a letter of condolence.

TRAVELERS. A woman visiting a place for a length of time should mail to her friends a visiting-card which contains her temporary address.

A man in similar situation should call upon his friends, and if he does not find them at home, should leave his card.

WEDDING INVITATIONS. Those present at the ceremony should leave cards for those inviting them, and if this is not possible, they can be sent by mail or messenger.

Those invited but not present should send cards.

WIDOW. See WIDOWS--CARDS.

WIFE. Only the wife of the oldest member of the oldest branch may use her husband's name without the initials.

WOMEN. Mrs. or Miss should always be used before the names. The cards of single women are smaller than those of married women.

The husband's name should be used in full, unless too long, when the initials are used. Only the wife of the oldest member of the oldest branch may use her husband's name without initials.

Reception days should appear in the lower left-hand corner, limiting dates--

as, Until Lent, or in January, may be either engraved or written.

If a special function is allotted to any reception days--as, the entertaining of special guests--the hour of the reception day may be written above the day and the date beneath it.

DAUGHTERS. See DAUGHTERS--CARDS.

LEAVING IN PERSON--BIRTH, ANNOUNCEMENT OF. If wishing to send congratulations, after receipt of a birth announcement card, cards should be left in person or sent by a messenger; cut flowers may be sent with the card.

Before the wedding cards are issued, an engaged woman should leave her card personally upon her friends without entering the house.

When calling at the beginning of the season a woman should leave her own card, those of the men of the family, and two of her husband's.

After formal invitations, a woman should leave her own card and those of the men of the family who were invited, whether they attended or not.

When calling formally a woman should leave a card, whether the hostess is at home or not.

When a woman calls upon a well-known friend, it is not necessary to send up a card.

When making a call at a hotel or other public place, the name of the person called upon should be written in the upper left- hand corner of the card--as:

For Mrs. Jane Wilson

The corner of the card should not be turned down.

P. P. C. cards may be left in person or sent by mail upon departure from city, or on leaving winter or summer resort.

The corner of the card should not be turned down.

RECEPTION. At receptions a woman should leave the cards in the hall or hand them to the servant.

At a "coming-out reception" a woman should leave cards for the mother and daughter.

A married man returns his social obligations to women by personal calls, or his wife can do it for him by leaving his card with her own.

MOTHER AND DAUGHTER. After her debut the younger of the two daughters has no card of her own, as her full baptismal name appears on her mother's card beneath her name. A year after her first appearance she may have a card of her own.

When a mother leaves her daughter's card, it is for the hostess only.

If reception day appear on the mother's card, the daughters also receive on that date, as the daughters have no reception days of their own.

MOTHER AND SON. When a mother is calling, she can leave cards of her son for the host and hostess if it is impossible for him to do so himself.

A son entering society can have his cards left by his mother upon a host and hostess. Invitations to entertainments will follow.

RETURNING TO TOWN. Cards of the entire family should be sent by mail to all acquaintances when returning after a prolonged absence.

When using cards, if out of town, the place of a woman's permanent residence can be written on the card--thus: New York. Philadelphia.

SENDING BY MAIL OR MESSENGER. A woman visiting a place for a length of time should mail to her friends her visiting-card containing her temporary address.

P. P. C. cards may be sent by mail or messenger upon departure from city, or on leaving winter or summer resort.

After a change of residence the cards of the entire family should be sent out as soon as possible.

At the beginning of the season both married and single women should send their cards to all their acquaintances.

Visitors to town should send cards to every one whom they desire to see, with the address written on the cards.

For afternoon tea a visiting-card may be used. The hour for the tea is written or engraved over, and the date beneath the fixed day of the week. They may be sent by mail or messenger.

The cards of a debutante may be sent by mail or messenger.

Mourning cards should be sent to indicate temporary retirement from society. Later cards should be sent to indicate return to society.

AFTERNOON TEA. If a woman is unable to be present at an afternoon tea she should send her card the same afternoon.

WEDDING RECEPTION. When invitations have been received to the church but not to the wedding reception, cards should be sent to the bride's parents and to the bridal couple.

WOMEN--STYLE, TITLES. Women having titles should use them before the name--as, Reverend or Rev. Mrs. Smith. Physicians use Dr. before or M.D. after the name. Office hours and other professional matters are omitted on cards for social use. Husband's titles should never be used. The home address is put in the lower right-hand and the club address in the lower left-hand corner.

The card of the eldest daughter in society is simply Miss Wilson.

CARDS OF ADMISSION TO CHURCH WEDDINGS. These cards are used at all public weddings held in churches, and when they are used no one should be admitted to the church without one. They are sent with the wedding invitations.

CARRIAGES.

BALLS. See BALLS-CARRIAGES.

DANCES. See DANCES-CARRIAGES.

FUNERALS. See FUNERALS-CARRIAGES.

MEN. In a general way a man should provide a carriage when escorting a woman in evening dress to any function. If she does not wear evening dress, and they are going to an informal affair, it would be proper to take a street-car.

SUPPERS. See SUPPER AND THEATRE PARTIES--MEN--CARRIAGES.

THEATRES. See THEATRES AND OPERA PARTIES GIVEN BY MEN--CARRIAGES.

WOMEN. A woman accepting, with her mother's or chaperone's consent, a man's invitation to the theatre may, with propriety, request him not to provide a carriage unless full dress on her part is requested.

CATHOLIC PRIEST--HOW ADDRESSED. An official letter begins: Reverend and Dear Sir, and ends: I have the honor to remain your humble servant. A social letter begins: Dear Father Wilson, and ends: I beg to remain faithfully yours, The address on the envelope is: The Reverend John J. Wilson. But if he holds the degree of D.D. (Doctor of Divinity), the address is: Reverend John J. Wilson, D.D., or Reverend Dr. John J. Wilson.

CELERY is eaten with the fingers.

CHANGE OF RESIDENCE. WOMEN. After a change of residence, the cards of the entire family should be sent out as soon as possible.

CHAPERONE. A chaperone takes precedence of her charge in entering drawing or dancing rooms and on ceremonious occasions. At an entertainment both enter together, and the chaperone should introduce her protege to the hostess and to others. The two should remain together during the evening. In a general way the chaperon takes under her charge the social welfare of her protege.

BALLS. A mother should attend balls with her daughters, going and returning with them, and if she is not invited, it is in good taste for the daughters to decline the invitation. A father can act as escort, if need be, instead of the mother. A mother can delegate her powers to some one else when requested to act as a chaperone.

MEN CALLING. A man should ask the chaperone's permission to call upon her protege, and once it is granted no further permission is necessary. The chaperone should be present while a debutante receives male callers the first year, and when the first call is made she should be present throughout the evening and should decide as to the necessity of her presence during subsequent visits.

CARDS. A chaperone introducing and accompanying young women should leave her own card with that of her protege.

DANCES. The chaperone should give her permission to a man who desires to dance, promenade, or go to supper with her charge, who should not converse with him at length save at the chaperon's side, and the chaperon should accompany both to supper. If without an escort, the young woman may accept the invitation of her last partner before supper is announced.

INTRODUCTIONS. A man should never be introduced direct by card or letter to a young unmarried woman. If he desires to be introduced, the letter or card of introduction should be addressed to her chaperone or mother, who may then introduce him to the young woman if she deems it advisable.

At an entertainment a chaperone may ask a young man if he wishes to be introduced to the one under her care.

LETTERS OF INTRODUCTION. A man having a letter of introduction to a young woman should present it in person to the chaperone. If the latter is out when he calls, he should mail it to her, and she may then notify him when he may call, and should herself be present.

SUPPER, TEA, DINNER. A young woman receiving an invitation to a man's supper, tea, or dinner may accept if she has the consent of her mother or chaperone, and is assured that a chaperone will be present.

THEATRES. A chaperone's permission should be asked before a man's invitation to the theatre can be accepted. The chaperone can also accept, on behalf of her protege, invitations from men to theatre parties or suppers, if she too is invited.

The chaperone should be present at mixed theatre parties--one for small, and two or more for larger parties and suppers. The chaperones may use their own carriage to call for the guests, and then meet the men at the places of entertainment. The chaperone should say when the entertainment shall close.

UNABLE TO BE PRESENT. When a chaperone is unable to fulfill her duties, she may delegate them to another, provided it is agreeable to all concerned.

CHEESE is first cut into small bits, then placed on pieces of bread or cracker, and lifted by the fingers to the mouth.

CHINA WEDDING. This is the twentieth wedding anniversary, and is not usually celebrated; but if it is, the invitation may bear the words NO PRESENTS RECEIVED, and congratulations may be extended in accepting or declining the invitation. An entertainment is usually provided for. Any article of china is appropriate as a gift.

CHOIR-BOYS AT WEDDINGS. These form a brilliant addition to a church wedding, and when employed they meet the bridal party in the vestibule, and precede them to the altar, singing a hymn or other appropriate selection.

CHRISTENING.

DRESS. The mother wears an elaborate reception gown to the church, with white gloves and a light hat or bonnet.

If the ceremony is at the house, she can wear an elaborate tea-gown.

The guests wear afternoon or evening dress, according whether the ceremony comes before or after 6 P.M.

FLOWERS. A christening ceremony offers a good opportunity for the guests who desire to present flowers to the mother. This is not obligatory, however, and must remain a matter of personal taste.

GIFTS. A christening ceremony offers a good opportunity for the invited guests, if they desire, to send a present to the baby.

These should be sent a day or two before the ceremony, and if of silver should be marked with the child's name, initials, or monogram.

GUESTS. The invitations should be promptly answered.

At a church ceremony the guests, as they are few in number, assemble in the front pews.

At a large house christening the affair is conducted somewhat like an afternoon reception. Wine is drunk to the child's health, and the guests take leave of the hostess.

INVITATIONS are issued by the wife only to intimate friends, and should be promptly answered.

If the christening is made a formal entertainment, to take place in the drawing-room, the invitations may be engraved.

MEN. If the ceremony is in the afternoon they wear afternoon dress, but at an evening affair evening dress.

At an afternoon ceremony in the summer it is allowable for the men to wear straw hats and light flannel suits.

At a large house christening the affair should be conducted somewhat like a reception, and men on departing should take leave of the hostess.

WOMEN dress as they would for an afternoon reception if the ceremony comes in the afternoon, and if it comes after breakfast or luncheon, as they would for a breakfast or luncheon.

At a large house christening the affair should be conducted like a reception, and women should take leave of the hostess on their departure.

CHURCH. A man usually follows the woman, who leads to the pew, and he enters after her, closing the door as he does so.

He should find the places in the service book for her.

This same courtesy he should extend to a woman who is a stranger to him.

CLERGYMAN.

CHRISTENING FEES. It is customary to send a fee to the officiating clergyman, unless he is a relative or a near friend.

EVENING DRESS. Custom permits a clergyman to wear his clerical dress at all functions at which other men wear evening dress; or, if he wishes, he may also wear the regulation full dress. The wearing of either is a matter of taste.

HOW ADDRESSED. All mail and correspondence should be addressed to Rev. Mr. Smith, but in conversation a clergyman should be addressed as Mr. Smith. If he has received the degree of D.D. (Doctor of Divinity)from some educational institution, then he is addressed as Dr. Smith, and his mail should be addressed as Rev. Dr. Smith.

WEDDING CEREMONY. The officiating clergyman (minister or priest) is selected by the bride, who usually chooses her family minister, and the latter is then called upon by the groom with regard to the details. If a very intimate friend or relative of the groom is a clergyman, it is in good taste for the bride to ask him either to officiate or to assist. If from any cause--as, living outside the State--the clergyman is unable to legally perform the ceremony, a magistrate should be present to legalize the ceremony, and should receive a fee.

CARRIAGE. A carriage should be provided by the groom to take the clergyman to the church, then to the reception, and thence to his house.

FEE. A fee should be paid the clergyman by the groom through the best man, who should hand it to him immediately after the ceremony. If two or three clergymen are present and assist, the fee of the officiating clergyman is double that of the others. The clergyman should receive at least five dollars in gold, clean bills, or check, in a sealed envelope, or more, in proportion to the groom's financial condition and social position.

WEDDING RECEPTION. The clergyman should always be invited to the reception.

CLUB.

ADDRESS. If residing at a club, a man's visiting- card should have his club's name in the lower right-hand corner; if not, the name should be put in lower left-hand corner.

STATIONERY. This is always in good form for social correspondence by men.

COACHING. See DRIVING.

COACHMAN-TIPS. It is customary when a guest leaves a house party after a visit to give the coachman a tip.

COLLEGE DEGREES. Custom, good taste, and the fitness of things forbid a college man having engraved, on his visiting-card, his college degrees--as, A.B., A.M., etc.

COMMERCE, Secretary of--How Addressed. An official letter begins: Sir, and ends: I have, sir, the honor to remain your most obedient servant. A social letter begins: My dear Mr, Wilson, and ends: I have the honor to remain most sincerely yours. The address on the envelope is: Hon. John J. Wilson, Secretary of Commerce.

COMMITTEES-PUBLIC BALLS. Public balls are conducted like private ones, and the etiquette is the same for the guests. The difference in their management is that, in place of a hostess, her functions and duties are filled by committees selected by the organization giving the ball.

CONCLUSION OF A LETTER. The standard conclusions of letters are: I remain sincerely yours, or; Believe me faithfully yours.

For business correspondence the standard conclusions are: Yours truly, or; Very truly yours.

For relatives and dear friends the standard forms are: Affectionately yours, or; Devotedly yours.

One should avoid signing a letter with only initials, Christian name, surnames, or diminutives.

MEN. In writing formally on business to a woman he knows slightly, a man could say: I am respectfully yours. When not on business he could write: I beg to remain yours to command.

He should avoid a signature like: J. Jones Wilson, but write: James J. Wilson

WOMEN. In social correspondence a married woman should sign: Minnie Wilson, and not: Mrs. John Wilson. If she wants to make known in a business letter the fact of her being married, and may not know if the person addressed knows the fact, she may write: Minnie Wilson (Mrs. John Wilson) An unmarried woman would sign her name as: Minnie Wilson, and if wishing not to be taken for a widow would sign: Miss Minnie Wilson.

CONDOLENCE.

CALLS. When death occurs in the family of a friend, one should call in person and make kindly inquiries for the family and leave a card, but should not ask to see those in trouble unless a very near and dear acquaintanceship warrants.

For a very intimate acquaintance, cut flowers may be left in person or sent, together with a card, unless the request has been made to send none.

CARDS. A visiting-card is used with the word CONDOLENCE written on it, and should be left in person if possible, but may be sent or mailed to intimate friends only if accompanied by a note of apology. If out of town, it should be sent by mail with letter of condolence.

A MR. and MRS. card may be used at any time for condolence, except for intimate friends.

LETTERS. Only the most intimate and dear friends should send letters of condolence, and they may send flowers with the note unless the request has been made to send none.

CONGRATULATIONS.

BIRTH, ANNOUNCEMENT OF. If wishing to send congratulations after a birth, cards should be left in person or sent by messenger. Cut flowers may be sent with the card.

CARDS. A MR. and MRS. card can be used at any time for congratulations. If left in person, which is preferable, the card should be accompanied by a kindly message, and, if sent by mail or messenger' the word CONGRATULATIONS should be written on it. Business and professional men are not required to make personal calls, and so may send their cards. A Mr. and Mrs. card can be used for all but near friends.

When a card is left in person, with a message of congratulations, nothing should be written thereon.

A man may mail his card to a woman engaged to be married, if acquaintance warrants the action.

Congratulations upon the birth of a child may be expressed by a man to its father by sending a card with the word Congratulations written on it, or by leaving it in person.

A card should be mailed to a man engaged to be married.

WEDDINGS. Congratulations may be sent with letter of acceptance or declination to a wedding to those sending the invitations. And if acquaintance with bride and groom warrant, a note of congratulations may be sent to them also.

Guests in personal conversation with the latter give best wishes to the bride and congratulations to the groom.

WEDDING ANNIVERSARIES. In accepting or declining invitations to wedding anniversaries, congratulations may be extended.

CONVERSATION AT DINNERS. Aim at bright and general conversation, avoiding all personalities and any subject that all cannot join in. This is largely determined by the character of the company. The guests should accommodate themselves to their surroundings.

COOKS-TIPS. It is customary for men who have been guests at a house party when they leave to remember the cook by sending her a tip.

CORN ON THE COB is eaten with the fingers of one hand. A good plan is to cut off the kernels and eat them with the aid of a fork.

CORNER OF CARD TURNED DOWN. This is no longer done by persons when calling and leaving cards.

CORRESPONDENCE. How to address official and social letters. See under title of person addressed --as, ARCHBISHOP, etc.

COSTUME BALLS.--INVITATIONS. Invitations are similar to invitations to balls, except that they have in place of DANCING in the lower left-hand corner. COSTUME OF THE XVIIIth CENTURY, BAL MASQUE, OR BAL POUDRE.

COTILLIONS. Germans are less formal than balls. Supper precedes the dancing. Those who do not dance or enjoy it can leave before that time.

The etiquette is the same as for balls.

DRESS. The regulation evening dress is worn.

HOSTESS. The rules governing a hostess when giving a ball are the same for a cotillion, with this addition--that there should be an even number of men and women, and, failing this, more men than women.

It is for the hostess to choose the leader of the cotillion, and to him are entrusted all its details.

At the conclusion of the cotillion the hostess stands at the door with the leader at her side, to receive the greetings and the compliments of the guests.

See also BALLS--HOSTESS.

INVITATIONS. The invitations are engraved, and the hour for beginning is placed in the lower left-hand corner, and are sent out two weeks in advance. They may be sent in one envelope.

Such invitations should be promptly accepted or declined.

COTILIONS BY SUBSCRIPTIONS. These are given by leading society women, who subscribe to a fund sufficient to pay all expenses of the entertainment.

They are usually held in some fashionable resort where suitable accommodations can be had.

Guests are shown to the cloak-room, where attendants check their wraps.

After the supper, the German, or cotillion, begins. Those not dancing in this generally retire. When leaving, guests should take leave especially of the patroness inviting them.

DRESS. Full dress is worn by all.

INVITATIONS. The patronesses whose names appear on the back of the cards are the subscribers. They send out the invitations to their friends. A presentation card, to be shown at the door, is sent with the invitation.

MEN. Men wear evening dress.

The men wait upon their partners and themselves at the table, the waiters assisting, unless small tables are used, when the patronesses sit by themselves, and others form groups as they like. The guests are served by the waiters, as at a dinner.

When retiring, guests should take leave especially of the patroness inviting them.

PATRONESSES. The patronesses stand in line to receive the guests, bowing or shaking hands as they prefer.

When supper is announced, the leading patroness leads the way with her escort, the others following. If small tables are used, the patronesses sit by themselves.

WOMEN. Women wear full dress.

When guests depart, they should take leave especially of the patroness inviting them.

COUNTESS--HOW ADDRESSED. An official letter begins: Madam, and ends: I have the honor to remain your Ladyship's most obedient servant. The address on the envelope is: To the Right Honorable The Countess of Kent.

A social letter begins: Dear Lady Kent, and ends: Believe me, dear Lady Kent, sincerely yours.

The address is: To the Countess of Kent.

COUNTRY CALLS. The usual rule in calling is for the residents to call first upon the temporary cottage people, and between these latter the early comers call first upon those coming later.

In the city there is no necessity for neighbors to call upon each other.

CRACKERS should be broken into small pieces and eaten with the fingers.

CRESTS. If men and women wish, these may be stamped in the latest fashionable colors on their stationery. It is not customary to use a crest and a stamped address on the same paper.

The present fashion in crests is that they should be of small size.

It is not usual to stamp the crest on the flap of the envelope.

If sealing-wax is used, some dull color should be chosen.

A person should avoid all individual eccentricities and oddities in stamping, such as facsimile autographs, etc.

CRYSTAL WEDDINGS. This anniversary comes after fifteen years of married life, and the invitations may bear the words: No presents received, and on their acceptance or declination, congratulations may be extended. An entertainment should be provided for. Any article of crystal or glass is appropriate as a gift.

DANCES.

CARRIAGES. A man should secure his carriage-check when leaving his carriage. It is safer to take wraps and coats to the house in case of accidents.

When taking a woman wearing evening dress to a ball or dance, a man should pro- vide a carriage.

DEBUTANTE. See DANCES--WOMEN--DEBUTANTE.

DRESS. Evening dress is worn by men and women.

DINNER INVITATIONS. The hostess issues two sets of invitations--one for those invited to both dinner and dance, and one for those invited to the dance only.

For the former, the hostess should use her usual engraved dinner cards, with the written words: Dancing at eleven, and for the latter her usual engraved At Home cards, with the written words: Dancing at eleven.

A less formal way is to use, instead of the At Home card, a Mr. and Mrs. card, or Mrs. And Miss card, with the following written in the lower left-hand corner: Dancing at ten. March the second. R. S. V. P.

INVITATIONS. These should be acknowledged by an acceptance, or declined, with a note of regret within one week.

MEN. ASKING A WOMAN TO DANCE. A man asks for the privilege of a dance, either with the daughter of the hostess or with any guest of the latter or any young woman receiving with her.

On being introduced to a woman, he may ask her for a dance, and he should be prompt in keeping his appointment.

It is her privilege to end the dance, and, when it is ended, he should conduct her to her chaperone, or, failing that, he should find her a seat--after which he is at perfect liberty to go elsewhere.

If for any cause a man has to break his engagements to dance, he should personally explain the matter to every woman with whom he has an engagement and make a suitable apology.

DEBUTANTE. At a debutante's reception the first partner is selected by the mother, usually the nearest and dearest friend, who dances but once, and the others follow.

INVITATIONS. Invitations to balls or assemblies should be answered immediately; if declined, the ticket should be returned. A man should call or leave cards a few days before the affair.

SUPPER. At balls and assemblies where small tables are provided, a man should not sit alone with his partner, but make up a party in advance, and keep together.

If a patroness asks a man to sit at her table, she should provide a partner for him.

At supper the senior patroness leads the way, escorted by the man honored for the occasion.

If one large table is provided, the men, assisted by the waiters, serve the women. When small tables are used the patronesses generally sit by themselves, and the guests group themselves to their own satisfaction.

TRONESSES. Their duties are varied and responsible--among them, the subscription to the expenses of the entertainments.

The patronesses should be divided into various committees to attend to special duties --as, music, caterers, supper arrangements, the ball-room, and all other details.

While affairs of this kind could be left in the hands of those employed to carry out the details, it is better and safer for each committee to follow the various matters out to the smallest details.

Those devising new features and surprises for such an occasion will give the most successful ball.

The one most active and having the best business ability should take the lead.

Lists should be compared, in order to avoid duplicate invitations.

The tickets should be divided among the patronesses, who, in turn, distribute them among their friends.

The patronesses should be at the ball-room in ample time before the arrival of the guests, to see that all is in readiness.

They should stand together beside the entrance to welcome the guests. They should see, as far as possible, that the proper introductions are made, and that every one is enjoying the evening, their own pleasure coming last.

If time permits, a hasty introduction to the patroness beside her may be made by a patroness, but it should not be done if there is the slightest possibility of blocking up the entrance.

A nod of recognition here and there, or a shake of the hands with some particular friend, is all that is necessary. Prolonged conversation should be avoided.

A patroness should not worry over the affair, or leave anything to be done at the last minute. If she has to worry, she should not show it, lest she interfere with the pleasure of others.

They should be the last to leave as well as the first to arrive, to see that the affair closes brilliantly.

SUPPER. The senior patroness leads the way to supper, escorted by the man honored for the occasion.

If one large table is provided, the men, assisted by the waiters, serve the women. When small tables are used, the patronesses generally sit by themselves, and the guests group themselves to their own satisfaction.

If a patroness asks a man to sit at her table, she should provide a partner for him, and in case of a previous engagement, he should notify her by mail.

WOMEN. A woman should always keep any engagement made, if possible. If, for a good reason, it is desired to break one, she should do so in ample time to enable the man to secure a partner.

It is bad form to refuse one partner for a dance and to accept another for the same dance afterward. After refusing to dance, a woman should lose that dance unless previously engaged.

A woman may refuse to dance at a public entertainment.

A young woman chaperoned should not accept a man's invitation, unless he first asks permission of her chaperone.

It is not good taste to keep late hours at an informal dance.

In round dances the man supports the woman with his right arm around the waist, taking care not to hold her too closely. Her right hand is extended, held by his left hand, and her left hand is on his arm or shoulder, her head erect.

When tired, the woman should indicate a desire to stop dancing.

When the dancing ends, the woman takes her partner's arm and strolls about a few minutes. He then conducts her to her seat by her chaperone, and, after a few remarks, excuses himself.

When supper is announced, and the young woman and her chaperone are in conversation with the man who danced with her last, they should accept his offer as escort if they are not already provided with one.

If a woman is without escort when supper is announced, she must rely upon attendants or members of the host's family.

At balls and assemblies where small tables are provided for the supper, the woman should not sit alone at a table with her partner, but she should have others present also.

DEBUTANTE. At a debutante's reception the first partner is selected by the mother, usually the nearest and dearest friend, who dances but once with her, and the others follow.

DANCES (FORMAL).

HOST. When supper is announced, the host leads the way with his partner, followed by hostess and escort, the rest following.

HOSTESS. She should limit the number of guests to the capacity of the house.

Invitations should include more men than women, for some men may not attend, and of those who do come, some may not dance.

An awning and carpet should be spread from curb to steps. The man stationed at the curb should open carriage doors for arriving and departing guests, distribute carriage- checks, and tell the drivers at what hour to return.

The servant opening the door directs the guests to their respective dressing-rooms.

A small orchestra should be provided and concealed behind palms or flowers.

In the absence of polished floors, carpets should be covered with linen crash, tightly and securely laid, in order to stand the strain of dancing.

Friends may assist in taking care of the guests, making introductions, etc.

SUPPER. Supper may be served at one large table or many small ones, as desired.

DANCES (INFORMAL). Dances of this character lack all possible formality. The invitations may be written or verbal.

Piano music is all that is required, played by one of the family or a professional.

Refreshments of a suitable nature are provided.

See also Chaperone. Dances.

DANCING.

INTRODUCTIONS. The man must be introduced to the woman, and should ask her for the pleasure of a dance.

MEN. A man should greet the host as soon as possible after seeing the hostess.

At any function where patronesses are present, a man should bow to the one inviting him, and give her a few words of greeting.

At balls all men should dance, and those who do not, have no place there, though invited.

If a man comes alone and has no partner, he should seek hostess or assistants, and request an introduction to women who dance.

After a dance a man should take a short stroll about the room with his partner before returning to her chaperone. Before retiring he may converse with her in general terms, from which he should have refrained previously.

A man escorting one or more women should see that they are cared for when supper is announced.

A man in conversation with a woman when supper is announced, if she is not engaged, may offer to take her into supper. Her chaperone should be invited at the same time.

Introductions should be made as much as possible before the dancing begins.

If introduced to a young woman, and she is free of engagement for the next dance, the man should invite her to dance.

Before asking a chaperoned woman to dance, the man should ask permission of her chaperone.

A man should pay especial attention to the women of the house, and invite them to dance as early as possible.

A man should seek out those women who, for some reason, are neglected by selfish men, especially unmarried women, and invite them to dance.

Men should keep engagements a few minutes before each dance.

If for some good reason it is desired to break an engagement, it should be done so as to leave ample time for the other to secure a partner for that dance.

In round dances, the man supports the woman with right arm about her waist, taking care not to hold her too closely. His left hand holds her right one, both extended.

The woman should indicate when she desires to stop dancing.

All persons should be at a formal dance not later than half an hour after the hour set.

A man should secure his carriage-check. It is safer to take wraps and coats to the house in case of accidents.

GLOVES. Gloves should be worn at formal dances, and should be put on before entering the room.

SHAKING HANDS. It is not customary to shake hands at formal dances.

SMOKING. Smoking should not be allowed in the dressing-room, but a special room should be provided. Men who dance should not smoke until leaving the house.

WOMEN. The time for the formal dance is indicated on the invitation, and all should be there not later than half an hour after the time set.

At private dances the maid takes and calls for the young woman in the absence of a male escort.

Young women should be chaperoned at all formal dances by their mother or others.

Introductions should be made as much as possible before the dancing begins.

DAUGHTERS.

CARDS. The card of the eldest daughter in society is simply Miss Wilson, and upon her death or marriage the card of the next daughter becomes the same. Where there are unmarried aunts and cousins having the father's name, only the eldest daughter of the eldest man can use the form Miss Wilson.

If two or more sisters enter society at about the same time, their names may appear on their mother's card as The Misses Wilson.

The name of the younger daughter should appear in full on her mother's card--as, Miss Mary Jane Wilson.

Until the younger daughter has formally, made her debut, she visits only intimate friends of the family. After her debut she has no card, and her full baptismal name appears on her mother's card, beneath her name, and not until a year or two after her first appearance does she have a card of her own.

When a mother leaves her daughter's card, it is for the hostess only.

If reception days appear on the mother's card, the daughters also receive on that day, as they have no reception date of their own.

After an entertainment the cards of the family may be left for the host and hostess by the eldest daughter.

The eldest daughter has her own circle of acquaintances, and can visit and receive independently of her mother.

DUTIES AT BALLS. See BALLS--DUTIES OF DAUGHTERS.

DAUGHTER OF BARON--HOW ADDRESSED. An official letter begins: Madam, and ends: I have the honor to remain, Madam, your obedient servant.

A social letter begins: Dear Miss Wilson, and ends: Believe me, I remain sincerely yours.

The envelope addressed to the eldest daughter reads: To the Honorable Miss Wilson, but to a younger daughter: To the Honorable Minnie Wilson.

DAUGHTER OF DUKE--HOW ADDRESSED. An official letter begins: Madam, and ends: I have the honor to remain your Ladyship's most obedient servant.

The address on the envelope is: To the Right Honorable the Lady Jane F. Wilson.

A social letter begins: Dear Lady Jane, and ends: Believe me, dear Lady Jane, very faithfully yours.

The address is: To the Lady Jane F. Wilson.

DAUGHTERS OF EARL--HOW ADDRESSED. An official letter begins: Madam, and ends: I have the honor to remain your Ladyship's most obedient servant.

The address on the envelope is: To the Right Honorable the Lady Jane F. Wilson.

A social letter begins: Dear Lady Jane, and ends: Believe me, dear Lady Jane, very faithfully yours.

The address is: To the Lady Jane F. Wilson.

DAUGHTER OF MARQUIS--HOW ADDRESSED. An official letter begins: Madam, and ends: I have the honor to remain your Ladyship's most obedient servant.

The address on the envelope is: To the Right Honorable the Lady Jane F. Wilson.

A social letter begins: Dear Lady Jane, and ends: Believe me, dear Lady Jane, very faithfully yours.

The address is: To the Lady Jane F. Wilson.

DAUGHTER OF VISCOUNT--HOW ADDRESSED. An official letter begins: Madam, and ends: I have the honor to remain, madam, your obedient servant.

A social letter begins: Dear Miss Wilson, and ends: Believe me, Miss Wilson, sincerely yours.

The envelope addressed to the eldest daughter would read: To the Honorable Miss Wilson, but to a younger daughter: To the Honorable Minnie Wilson.

DAYS AT HOME. Only very intimate persons should call on any other days than those named on an At Home card.

DAY OF WEDDING. The wedding-day is named by the bride, and her mother's approval is asked by the groom.

DEATH IN THE FAMILY. Cards, writing-paper, and envelopes should be bordered in black. The announcement of the death may be printed or engraved, preferably the latter. Full name of deceased, together with date of birth and death, and residence, should be given.

The frequenting of places of amusements, entertainments, or social functions should not be indulged in for at least a year if in mourning for near relatives.

CONDOLENCE. After a death in the family of an acquaintance, a card with the word Condolence written on it should be left in person or by messenger. For very intimate acquaintances, cut flowers may be left in person or sent, together with a card or letter, unless request has been made not to do so.

DEBUTANTE. A debutante should make her debut between the ages of seventeen and twenty, and should not appear at any public function before her debut. She should be thoroughly versed in the laws of good society. She should be extremely cautious at all times in her dealings with men. She should follow, without reserve, the advice of mother or chaperone. She should avoid forwardness, and be quiet in manner and in speech. Men acquaintances should be carefully chosen, and great care exercised in accepting invitations from them.

AFTERNOON TEAS (FORMAL). When a tea is given in honor of a debutante, she stands beside the hostess (usually her mother), and each guest is introduced to her. Flowers should be liberally provided, and friends may contribute on such an occasion.

A debutante should not make any formal visits alone the first year, and should not receive men visitors unless her chaperone is present. Should a man call during the first season, and neither her mother nor her chaperone be present, she should decline the visit. She may make and receive visitors alone the second season.

When calling upon a debutante, men and women should leave cards for her and her mother.

CARDS. A debutante should use her mother's card with her name engraved under her mother's, but after a season she uses her own card. Personal cards should not be used during the first season. If she is the eldest unmarried daughter, her name is engraved (as, Miss A--) beneath her mother's name, but if there are other sisters, with the initials (as, Miss A. A--).

The cards of a debutante may be sent by mail or messenger.

DANCES. A debutante always receives with her mother standing by her side. A good order is for the mother to stand nearest the door, the debutante next, and the father last.

It is a good plan for the debutante to ask a few of her girl friends to stand beside her the first half hour.

The mother should introduce guests to her daughter, who may introduce them to her friends.

The debutante shakes hands with each one introduced to her. She dances every dance, and at the end stands beside her mother to receive the greetings of the guests.

The girls standing up with the debutante after the first hour are free to dance and enjoy themselves as they please without standing in line again.

MEN. Her mother should select in advance the man who is to have the pleasure of the first dance with the debutante at her debut. No man should dance more than once with the debutante. If well acquainted with the family, a man may send flowers to a debutante at the time of her first debut. A man should make a formal call on mother and daughter a day or two after her debut, and, if unable to do so, he should send a card.

DEBUT. When her mother receives visits after her debut, the daughter is included, and should be present. The mother should keep a complete record of the visits made by entering the cards in a book kept for that purpose.

FLOWERS. Friends should send flowers to a debutante at a formal tea given in her honor.

MEN. When calling upon a debutante, a man should leave cards for her and her mother, whether the entertainment was attended or not.

See also DEBUTS.

DEBUTS. A debut may be made at a dinner, reception, or ball. The debutante's card should be enclosed with the invitation, reading: Miss Wilson; or, if a younger daughter, Miss Minnie Wilson. For an "At Home" debut, the least formal of all these entertainments, the name of the debutante is engraved below that of her mother.

The mother and elder unmarried sisters prior to the debut should call formally upon those whom they wish to invite to the ceremony. Cards of the family are left, including those of father and brothers.

BALLS--INVITATIONS. When a young woman is to be introduced into society by a ball given in her honor, the parents may use a Mr. and Mrs. calling card, with the words added in writing: Dancing at ten o'clock, with card of the debutante enclosed.

Or the parents may use a specially engraved invitation.

CARDS, LEAVING. At the entertainments at a debut, as at a supper, cards should be left for the mother and daughter, and if guests are unable to be present, they should send them the day of the entertainment.

ENTERTAINMENTS. Debuts may be an "At Home," supper, or dinner, the latter being more formal, and only intimate friends being invited. When making her debut, the debutante should stand beside her mother in the drawing-room, near the door, and be introduced by her. On formal occasions the father stands with them. The debutante may receive flowers from intimate friends only.

AT HOMES. These are the least formal.

SUPPERS OR DINNERS. If the debut takes the form of a supper or dinner, the brother takes in the debutante, and the father the most distinguished woman; or, if there is no brother, he takes in the debutante himself, and she is seated at his left hand. The mother is escorted by the most distinguished man.

Should dancing follow, the mother should select the first partner, who dances but once, when others are at liberty to follow.

GUESTS. Guests should offer congratulations to a debutante at her debut in a few well-chosen words, and also to the parents. A few moments of conversation with her only is admissible.

INVITATIONS. Invitations are engraved, and should be sent by mail or messenger two weeks in advance, addressed to Mr. and Mrs. A, or Mrs. B, or The Misses A. While the invitations to a family may be enclosed in one envelope and sent to the principal one of the family, the son of the family should receive a separate invitation. Men should receive separate invitations and acknowledge them, in person.

Acknowledgment is mot necessary for an "At Home" debut occurring in the afternoon, but would be for a formal one in the evening, for which special engraved invitations had been sent.

If invitations for an afternoon "At Home" reception are accepted, cards should be left for mother and daughter. And, if not attending, cards should be sent by mail or messenger.

DIAMOND WEDDINGS. These occur after seventy- five years of married life, and naturally are of very rare occurrence. If they are celebrated, the invitation may bear the words: NO PRESENTS RECEIVED, and congratulations may be extended in accepting or declining the invitation. An entertainment should be provided for. Any article of diamonds or precious stones is appropriate as a gift.

DINNERS. If the circle of acquaintances is large, a series of dinners is necessary during the season.

Dinners should begin at an hour between seven-thirty and eight-thirty.

The dining-room should be bright and attractive, well lighted, and artistically decorated with flowers.

The success of a dinner lies in the selection of the guests, with regard to their congeniality to each other, and their conversational powers and varying attainments. It is better to have a few at a time, perhaps eight, as a larger number is unmanageable.

CALLS. Guests should call soon after the dinner.

DRESS. Full dress is worn by both men and women.

GUESTS. When guests are not congenial, or have dislikes, they should not show it, but appear as if the contrary were the case.

Guests should be prompt in arriving at the hour named.

At the table it is in good taste to accept whatever is offered, eating it or not, as one desires. Wines should be accepted, even if one does not partake of them. And if a toast is offered, a guest should recognize the courtesy by raising his glass.

Conversing across the table is permissible, provided the distance does not require the voice to be unduly raised.

When coffee is served in the drawing-room, young women serve, and the men hand it to the guests.

When the men re-enter the drawing-room after the coffee, the guests should retire, unless some further entertainment follows. This is usually about eleven o'clock. When leaving, a guest should thank the host and hostess, making some agreeable and appropriate remark suitable to the occasion.

HOST. When dinner is announced, the host offers his left arm to the woman he escorts. She may be the special invited guest, or the most prominent guest present.

The signal for all to rise is given by the hostess, who bows to the woman on the host's right. The men escort the women to the door or drawing-room, after which they return, and cigars and liquors are offered.

The host wears full dress.

GUEST LATE. The host should always come forward to shake hands with the late-comer, and help him to find his seat, and do all in his power to make his late-coming quickly overlooked.

HOSTESS. The hostess receives her guest at the parlor entrance.

At table the guests should remain standing until all have found their places, when the host and hostess seat themselves, after which the others follow.

The men should assist the women they escort before taking their own seats.

At an informal dinner a hostess should introduce a man to the woman he is to escort to dinner, informing him whether he is to sit on the right or left hand of the host.

When the dinner is announced the host with his escort leads the way, followed by the guests, and the hostess and her escort come last.

GUEST LATE. The hostess should always bow and shake hands with a guest arriving late, but does not rise unless the guest is a woman.

HOURS. Dinners begin from 7 to 8 P.M., and usually last from one hour to an hour and a half.

INTRODUCTIONS. If a man is not acquainted with the woman assigned to him, the hostess should introduce him to the woman.

INVITATIONS. These should be acknowledged immediately by a letter of acceptance, or declining with regret.

The invitations are given in the name of husband and wife, and should be sent out two or four weeks in advance. R. S. V. P. is not used, and they should be answered immediately.

Invitations to a dinner in honor of a special guest are engraved, and state this fact. If for good reasons there is not sufficient time to engrave, an ordinary invitation may be used, and a visiting-card enclosed, upon which is written: To meet Miss Wilson.

For ceremonious dinners, cards may be engraved, with place for guest's name left blank and filled in by hand.

When frequent dinners are given, invitations may be engraved, with blanks to be filled with dates, etc.

Written invitations are also proper to indicate an unceremonious dinner. Note sheets can be used.

HUSBAND AND WIFE. Both the husband and wife should always be invited to a dinner.

When a husband and wife are invited to dinner, and the former does not accept, the wife should decline, giving her reason. The hostess can then invite the wife only, who may accept.

MEN. Full dress is necessary for all except informal dinners.

The man at the door, after asking the guest's name, hands him an envelope, with his name upon it, enclosing a card with the name of the woman he is to escort to dinner; or these envelopes may be in the dressing- rooms, if preferred. It will also be designated at which side of the table (right or left) a man is to sit; or a diagram of the table, with the names of the guests, should be hung in each dressing-room. The guests pair off as indicated.

As soon as possible a man should seek the woman assigned to him, and inform her that he will be pleased to act as her escort, disguising any personal preference he may have otherwise.

He should offer his left arm when escorting her to dinner.

When the dinner is announced, the host leads the way with the woman he escorts, and the rest follow. To avoid confusion, a man should remember on which side of the table he is to sit, his place being indicated by a dinner card.

If unacquainted with the woman a man is to escort to dinner, he should seek an introduction from the hostess.

When the women rise to leave, the men rise and remain standing until the women leave the dining-room, or they may accompany them to the drawing-room, and then return for coffee and cigars. They should not remain longer than half an hour.

LEAVING CARDS. After a dinner a man should leave a card for host and hostess, whether the invitation was accepted or not; or it may be sent by mail or messenger, with an apology for so doing.

PRECEDENCE. The host offers his right arm to the woman who is the guest, or the most distinguished woman, or the eldest, or the one invited for the first time. If the dinner is given in honor of a married couple, the host would take in the wife, and the husband would accompany the hostess, who comes last in the procession into the dining-room.

It is a fixed rule that relatives, or husbands and wives, are never seated together.

If possible, there should be an equal number of men and women, and if the latter outnumber the former, the hostess enters alone.

SECOND HELPING. At formal dinner parties, luncheons, and breakfasts, second helpings are never offered by the host or hostess, and should not be asked for by the guests. This is only permissible at a small dinner party or at the daily family meal.

Of course, this does not apply to a second glass of water for which the guest might ask, or for wine, for which the butler should keep a good lookout.

TABLE ETIQUETTE. See TABLE ETIQUETTE.

WOMEN. When wraps have been removed, and the woman leaves the dressing-room, the escort chosen by the hostess approaches and makes known the fact, accompanying her to the table. If the escort is not thoroughly agreeable to the woman, she should conceal the fact.

At the conclusion of a dinner the hostess rises and the women follow, leaving their napkins unfolded. They retire to the drawing-room, while the men remain for coffee and cigars. If the men prefer, they may escort them to the drawing-room, where they bow and return.

GLOVES. Women may remove their gloves at table, and it is not necessary to replace them. They should be laid in the lap. The hostess generally determines whether the women should resume their gloves or not by her own actions.

Full dress is worn.

GIVEN BY MEN--WOMEN. A young woman may accept a man's invitation, provided she has the consent of her mother or guardian, and is assured that there will be present a chaperone.

GIVEN BY BACHELORS. See BACHELORS' DINNERS.

DINNER DANCE.

INVITATIONS. The hostess issues two sets of invitations--one for those invited to both the dinner and the dance, and one for those invited to the dance only.

For the former she could use her usual engraved dinner cards with the words: Dancing at eleven, and for the latter her usual engraved At Home cards with the words: Dancing at eleven.

A less formal way for the latter invitation is to use the Mr. and Mrs. card or Mrs. and Miss card, and to write on it in the lower left hand corner: Dancing at ten, February the tenth.

DOCTOR--HOW ADDRESSED. A doctor or physician should be addressed as Dr. both by correspondence and in conversation.

This title of Dr. must not be confounded with the honorary degree of Doctor of Divinity, conferred upon clergymen by educational institutions, and the degree of Doctor of Philosophy, conferred upon college professors after certain conditions of study have been complied with.

DOWAGER DUCHESS. See DUCHESS, DOWAGER.

DOWAGER MARCHIONESS. See MARCHIONESS, DOWAGER.

DRESS.

AFTERNOON. See AFTERNOON--DRESS.

AFTERNOON TEAS. See AFTERNOON TEAS--DRESS.

AT HOMES. See AT HOMES--DRESS.

BACHELORS' DINNERS. See BACHELOR'S DINNERS-- DRESS.

BACHELORS' TEAS. See BACHELOR'S TEAS--DRESS.

BALLS. See BALLS--DRESS.

BREAKFASTS. See BREAKFASTS--DRESS.

CHRISTENINGS. See CHRISTENING--DRESS.

COTILLIONS. See COTILLIONS--DRESS.

COTILLIONS BY SUBSCRIPTIONS. See COTILLIONS BY SUBSCRIPTIONS--DRESS.

DANCES. See DANCES--DRESS.

DINNERS. See DINNERS--DRESS.

EVENING. See EVENING DRESS.

GARDEN PARTIES. See GARDEN PARTIES--DRESS.

HIGH TEAS. See HIGHT TEAS--DRESS.

HOUSE PARTIES. See HOUSE PARTIES--DRESS.

LUNCHEONS. See LUNCHEONS--DRESS.

MATINEES. See MATINEES--DRESS.

MUSICALES. See MUSICALES--DRESS.

THEATRES. See THEATRES--DRESS.

WEDDINGS. See WEDDINGS--DRESS.

DRESS--MEN AND WOMEN. For particulars as to dress at different functions, see each entertainment --as, Balls, Dinners, At Homes, Theatres, Breakfasts, etc.

DRESS--WOMEN.

BRIDE. See BRIDE--DRESS.

BRIDESMAIDS. See BRIDESMAIDS--DRESS.

CALLS. See CALLS--WOMEN--DRESS.

FUNERALS. See FUNERALS--WOMEN--DRESS.

MAID OF HONOR. See MAIDOF HONOR--DRESS.

MOURNING. See MOURNING--DRESS, WOMEN.

DRESSING-ROOMS. At all entertainments, dressing-rooms should be provided for both the men and for the women, with suitable attendants, where all outer wraps, coats, over- shoes, etc., should be left.

DRIVING

MEN. When driving with a woman, a man should be careful that the carriage is well drawn up to the steps, and that she be given time in which to comfortably seat herself before he begins to drive.

A man when driving with a woman should refrain from asking her permission to smoke, and, of course, would never do so without her permission.

He should be careful to lift his hat as if he were on the street, and if this is not possible, to touch it with the whip in place of a bow.

The host of a coaching party, if he is also the whip, would give the chaperone the seat on the box at the left of his, unless he wished that seat to be occupied by some special young woman. The person occupying this seat should always be helped by the host to climb to her place.

It is customary when the coach is a high one to seat a woman between two men, and they would ascend and descend in the order in which they were seated.

Even if the woman asks a man to drive with her, he should help her to her seat, and be ready to step down when a halt is made to assist her to alight.

It is not customary when a woman has asked a man to drive with her for her to call for him at his club or home, but to meet him at her house.

DRESS. The whip wears a gray suit with a gray high hat and gray gloves, with a white silk tie and white linen. But in summer this costume is often made lighter and more comfortable to suit the weather, and a straw hat or panama, with flannel trousers and dark serge sacque coat, would be in good taste.

There are no hard and fast rules governing the dress of men when driving.

WOMEN. The etiquette in general is the same for a woman as for a man.

When a woman asks a man or a male relative to drive with her, she does not call for him, but meets him at her door. Even if a groom is present, he should help her to mount to her seat, and at the proper time descend before her and help her to alight.

DUCHESS--HOW ADDRESSED. An official letter begins: Madam, may it please Your Grace, and ends: I have the honor to remain your Grace's obedient servant.

A social letter begins: My Dear Duchess of Kent, and ends: Believe me, dear Duchess, yours very truly.

The address on the envelope is: To Her Grace, The Duchess of Kent.

DUCHESS, DOWAGER--HOW ADDRESSED. An official letter begins: May it please YOUR Grace, and ends: I have the honor to remain your Graces's obedient servant.

A social letter begins: My dear Duchess Of Kent, and ends: Believe me, dear

Duchess, yours very truly.

The address on the envelope is: To Her Grace, The Dowager Duchess of Kent, or, To Her Grace, Minnie, Duchess of Kent.

DUKE--HOW ADDRESSED. An official letter begins: My Lord Duke, may it please your grace, and ends: I have the honor to be your grace's most obedient servant.

A social letter begins: My dear Duke of Kent, and ends: believe me, dear Duke, your Grace's very faithfully.

The address on the envelope is: To His Grace, The Duke of Kent.

DAUGHTER OF. See Daughter of Duke.

WIFE OF YOUNGER SON OF. See Wife of Younger Son of Duke.

YOUNGER SON OF. See Son (Younger) of Duke.

EARL--HOW ADDRESSED. An official letter begins: My Lord, and ends: I have the honor to be your lordship's obedient servant.

The address on the envelope is: To the Right Honorable The Earl Of Kent.

A social letter begins: Dear Lord Kent, and ends: Believe me my dear Lord Kent, very sincerely yours.

The address on the envelope is: To the Earl of Kent

DAUGHTER OF. See Daughter of Earl.

WIFE OF YOUNGER SON. See Wife of Younger Son of Earl.

YOUNGER SON OF. See Son (Younger) of Earl.

EGGS are usually broken into a glass and eaten with a spoon.

ELEVATOR. Men should remove their hats when riding in an elevator with women, although it is held by some that an elevator is as much a public conveyance as a car, and this act of courtesy as unnecessary in the one place as in the other. Women enter and leave before men.

ENGAGEMENT.

MEN It is his duty to see the woman's parents or guardian, and to make known his intentions, and to tell them fully and frankly about himself, his family, his social position, and business prospects. He should court the fullest investigation, and take his own family into his confidence, but not mention it to others.

PARENTS OF MAN. They should send their pleasant greetings and congratulations, accompanied with flowers, and if both families are old acquaintances, a present may be sent to the prospective bride.

PARENTS OF WOMAN. The first step is to bring together both parents in social intercourse-- as, by a dinner given by the man's or woman's family, when friends may be invited, by interchange of notes and congratulations, by any social visit, or by any function that good taste may dictate.

If one family lives out of town, it may invite various members of the other family living in the city to make visits of some duration, as a week or more. These visits should be returned.

PUBLIC ANNOUNCEMENT. This item of news is rarely published in the papers, but if it is, the expense is borne by the family of the woman. The public announcement is usually made at some social entertainment--as, a dinner, tea, or an "At Home," given by either family.

At a formal dinner given by the family of the woman, the father takes out his daughter first and her fiance escorts her mother. At the proper time the father drinks his future son-in-law's health and announces the engagement. All rise, and congratulations follow.

Notes may be written to intimate friends informing them of the happy event.

WOMEN. A woman should at once confide in her parents, and trust to their future guidance and to their making a full investigation of the man, his social condition, and business prospects. They should not mention the matter to others.

Immediately after the engagement, each of the two parties should be introduced to the family of the other party. Before the wedding-cards are issued the woman should leave her card personally at the homes of her friends, but without entering. After the wedding-cards are issued she should not appear at any social function, or make any personal visits, or be seen at any place of amusement.

It is not wise for her to call at the place of business of her fiance, and if a meeting is necessary, it is better to make an appointment elsewhere.

RING. The ring is given by the man immediately after the announcement of the engagement to the woman, who wears it on the third finger of her left hand. It should be a small and unostentatious one. Diamonds, rubies, moonstones, sapphires, and other precious stones may be used.

He may ask the woman to aid him in the selection, but it is better for him to make the selection alone. The woman may give the man an engagement ring or a gift if she wishes.

ENTERTAINMENTS--CALLS AFTER. See CALLS--MEN--AFTER ENTERTAINMENTS.

ENVELOPES, ADDRESSING. See ADDRESSING ENVELOPES.

ESQUIRE. Either ESQ. or MR. may be used in addressing a letter, but never the two at the same time.

EVENING CALLS. When no special day for receiving is indicated, calls may be made at any proper hour, according to the custom of the locality. Men of leisure may call at the fashionable hours, from two till five o'clock in the afternoon, while business and professional men may call between eight and nine in the evening, as their obligations prevent them from observing the fashionable hours.

EVENING DRESS.

Men. Evening dress should be worn on all formal occasions, consisting of the swallow- tail coat of black material, made in the prevailing fashion, with waistcoat and trousers of the same material; or a white vest may be worn.

The linen must be white. Studs or shirt- buttons may be worn, according to fashion. The collar should be high, and the cravat white. Low patent-leather shoes and white kid gloves complete the costume.

Evening dress should be worn at all formal functions after six o'clock--as, balls, dinners, suppers, receptions, germans, formal stag parties, theatre, opera, and fashionable evening calls where women are present.

The phrase, "evening dress," is now used in place of full dress.

A Tuxedo should never be worn when women are present.

See also TUXEDO. CLERGYMAN--EVENING DRESS.

WEDDINGS, EVENING. Full evening dress is worn by the groom and ushers.

Guests are likewise in evening dress.

CLERGYMAN. Custom permits a clergyman to wear his clerical dress at all functions where other men wear evening dress, or he may wear evening dress.

EVENING RECEPTIONS. The etiquette is the same as for an afternoon tea (formal), save that no cards are left by the guests, and that they wear evening dress.

See AFTERNOON TEAS (FORMAL).

FACSIMILE CARDS, engraved, are no longer used.

FAMILY OF BRIDE. The family, except the father, leave the house first, then the bridesmaids, the maid of honor with the mother, and last the bride with her father or nearest male relative. At church the family is seated by the ushers.

At the conclusion of the ceremony they are the first to be escorted from their pew and to take their carriage for the wedding reception or breakfast.

WEDDING BREAKFAST. The bride's father or her nearest male relative takes in the groom's mother, and the bride's mother, as hostess, is taken in by the groom's father.

WEDDING RECEPTION. The parents of both bride and groom stand up with the married couple, and are introduced to the guests.

FAMILY OF GROOM. At the church the family and relatives of the groom are seated on one side, while the family of the bride and her relatives are seated on the other.

WEDDING BREAKFAST. The groom's mother is taken in by the bride's father, and the groom's father takes in the bride's mother, who, acting as hostess, comes last.

WEDDING RECEPTION. The parents of both bride and groom stand up with the married couple, and are introduced to the guests.

FAREWELL BACHELOR DINNER. See BACHELOR'S FAREWELL DINNERS.

FAREWELL BRIDAL LUNCHEON. See BRIDE--FAREWELL LUNCHEON.

FATHER OF BRIDE.

DEBUTS. When the debut is a formal one, he stands beside his wife and daughter, and receives the congratulations of the guests. At a supper or dinner he escorts the most distinguished woman. If there is no brother to escort the debutante, he does so, and she is seated at his left hand.

DINNER, ENGAGEMENT. At a formal dinner given by the family of the engaged woman the father takes out his daughter first and her fiance escorts her mother. At the proper time the father drinks to the health of his future son-in-law, and announces the engagement. All rise, and congratulations follow.

He wears evening dress.

The father of the bride, or her nearest male relative, drives to the church with her, and is there received by the ushers and bridesmaids, and escorts her in the procession up the aisle.

After the procession has arrived at the chancel and the groom comes forward to take the bride's hand, he steps back a little way and waits for the clergyman's words: "Who giveth this woman away?" He then places the bride's right hand in that of the clergyman, and retires to his seat in the pew with his family.

WEDDING BREAKFAST. He takes in the mother of the groom, following the ushers and the maids of honor.

WEDDING RECEPTION. He escorts the groom's mother, and receives with the married couple.

FATHER OF GROOM. At a wedding breakfast he should take in the mother of the bride, and at a wedding reception he receives with the bride and groom.

At a church wedding he is, of course, given a front seat among those reserved for the groom's family.

He should wear afternoon dress for an afternoon wedding, and evening dress at an evening wedding.

FEES.

CHRISTENING. See CHRISTENING--FEES

WEDDING. The wedding fee, preferably gold or clean bills in sealed envelope, is given by the best man to the officiating clergyman. Custom leaves the amount to the groom, who should give at least five dollars or more, in proportion to his income and social position. The clergyman usually gives the fee to his wife.

A fee should also be paid to the sexton and the organist

FIANCE, MOURNING FOR. In the event of the death of a woman's betrothed shortly before the date of the wedding, she may wear black for a short period or full mourning for a year.

FINGER-BOWL. The fingers should be dipped in the water and gently rubbed together, and dried on the napkins.

FIRST CALLS. Newcomers and brides are called upon first.

After a country visit, the visitor should call first upon the hostess when the latter returns to town.

Other things being equal, the younger or unmarried woman calls first upon the older or married woman.

A woman returning to town before another one would make the first call.

If one woman issues her AT HOME card before another, she should receive the first call.

FISH should be eaten with a fork held in the right hand and a piece of bread held in the left hand. The bones should be removed from the mouth with the aid of a fork or with the fingers. If by the latter, great delicacy should be used.

FLOWER GIRL. The flower girls--one or two, as may be the case--follow the maid of honor up the isle and strew flowers in the path of the bride, who follows after.

In the procession down the isle they should follow the bride.

Flower girls and pages are not used now as much as formerly.

FLOWERS. Between friends, flowers may be sent as an expression of sympathy in either joy or sorrow.

BIRTH, ANNOUNCEMENT OF. If wishing to send congratulations after a birth, cards should be left in person or sent by a messenger. Cut flowers may be sent with the card.

BRIDE. If she wishes, a bride may present flowers to her bridesmaids, and also to the best man and ushers.

CHRISTENING. A christening ceremony offers a good opportunity for the guests who desire to present flowers to the mother. This is not obligatory, however, and must remain a matter of personal taste.

CONDOLENCE CALLS. When making a condolence call upon a very intimate friend, cut flowers may be left in person or sent, together with a card, unless request has been made to send none.

DEBUTANTE. Friends should send flowers to a debutante at a formal tea given in her honor.

ENGAGEMENT. Flowers should accompany the greetings from the parents of the man to the parents of the woman.

FUNERALS. See FUNERALS--FLOWERS.

GROOM. He pays for the bridal bouquet carried by the bride at the wedding ceremony, and, if he wishes, for the bouquets carried by the bridesmaids.

MEN. If well acquainted with a debutante's family, a man may send her flowers at the time of her debut.

After a slightly intimate acquaintance, a man can present flowers to a young unmarried woman as a token of sympathy either of joy or sorrow.

It is not usual for a man to send flowers to a woman who is a mere acquaintance.

BALLS. It is permissible for a man, if he wishes, to send flowers to a woman he is to escort to a ball.

THEATRE OR OPERA. It is permissible, but not necessary, for a man to send flowers to the woman he is to take to the theatre or to the opera.

WEDDING TRIP. The best man should arrange beforehand all the details of the trip--such as the tickets, parlor-car, flowers, baggage, etc.

PALL-BEARERS. See PALL-BEARERS--FLOWERS.

FORK AND KNIFE. See KNIFE AND FORK.

FORMAL AFTERNOON TEAS. See AFTERNOON TEAS (FORMAL).

FORMAL DANCES. See DANCES (FORMAL).

FRUIT. All raw fruit, except melons, berries, and grapefruit, are eaten with the fingers. Canned fruits are eaten with a spoon.

FULL DRESS. This phrase is now no longer in good usage, and instead should be used the term: "Evening Dress," which SEE.

FUNERALS. A member of the family, or very near relative, should take charge of the ceremony and direct the undertaker. A large funeral should be avoided, and the ceremony confined to the immediate family and nearest relatives, and, if possible, the service should be at the church.

All the details of the funeral should be carefully considered and carried out, with the ceremony started at the hour set, and with all appearance of confusion avoided.

It is not now customary to watch by the dead at night.

Funerals should be private, and only those intimately interested should be invited.

CARRIAGES. A carriage should always be provided to call for the clergyman and to take him from the church or cemetery back to his house. Carriages should also be provided to take the friends, mourners, and pall-bearers from the house to the church, and then to the cemetery and return. These are provided by the family.

DRESS. See FUNERALS--MEN.

EXPENSES. Though it is not customary for the clergyman in Protestant churches to expect or to receive fees for conducting funerals, yet it is in perfectly good taste to offer him a fee. In the Roman Catholic Church the rate of fees for funerals is fixed. There are, besides, fees for the sexton, the organist, and the singers.

FLOWERS. The family, in publishing notice of funeral, may add: "Kindly omit flowers." However, in the absence of such a notice, at the public funerals of prominent persons elaborate designs may be sent. But at a private funeral, if flowers are sent, they should be choice and delicate.

The custom is growing of having fewer flowers, and it is no longer in good taste to have a carriage in the procession carrying flowers and set pieces. A good use of the large set pieces is to send them afterward to the hospitals.

If any flowers are laid upon the grave they should be those given by the nearest relatives.

INVITATIONS. A church funeral can be attended by any one, friend or acquaintance, and no slight should be felt at the non-receipt of an invitation. Those attending should take especial pains to be in the church before the funeral procession arrives, and that they do nothing to distract from the solemnity of the occasion.

Notice of death and date of funeral may be printed on heavy bordered cards, or on mourning paper, and sent to friends. Sometimes a notice is written and sent to most intimate friends.

MEN--DRESS. A man should wear either a black frock coat or a black cutaway, with the necktie, gloves, and other parts of the dress as subdued as possible. Under no conditions should light ties or light-colored linen be worn.

PALL-BEARERS. See PALL-BEARERS.

PRECEDENCE. At a church funeral the parents, arm in arm, follow the body of their child, and the children come next in the order of their age.

A widow, leaning on the arm of her eldest son, follows the body of her husband, and the other children come after.

A widower, attended by his eldest daughter or son, follows the body of his wife, and the children come after.

The elder children always precede the younger. The pall-bearers are seated at the left of the main isle, and the near relatives at the right.

PUBLIC NOTICE. When the date of the funeral has been determined upon, notice should be published in the papers, giving date, place, and time of funeral--also date of birth and late place of residence of deceased. Such announcement may contain notice that the interment is private, and also the words: "Kindly omit flowers."

A notice of death and date of funeral may be printed on heavy bordered cards or mourning paper, and sent to friends. Sometimes a notice is written and sent to most intimate friends.

CHURCH. The pall-bearers and the nearest relatives meet at the house. At the appointed hour the procession leaves the house, the casket borne on the shoulders of the undertaker's assistants, followed by the pall-bearers, relatives, and friends.

The same order is followed in the procession up the aisle, the relatives occupying the first pews on the right, the pall-bearers the first pews on the left, of the middle aisle. At the conclusion of the ceremony the friends wait until the family and pall-bearers have left, and then quietly retire.

HOUSE. At a house funeral, some one representing the family should receive the people as they enter and direct them where to go, it being customary for the family and relatives to be in one room and the friends in another.

Usually there are no pall-bearers; but if there are, their duties are the same as at a church funeral. The clergyman should stand near the casket, and if there are musicians they should be so stationed that, while they are not seen, they are easily heard. At the conclusion of the ceremony the friends depart, and thus allow the family and relatives to take the last leave of the deceased before they take the carriages for the cemetery.

It is customary for the family to be in retirement at the hour of the funeral, and they are the first to enter the carriages.

Those in charge of the house should, after the funeral party has left, arrange the apartments to make them as cheerful as possible, and also provide a substantial meal for the mourners on their return.

GARDEN PARTIES.

CARDS. Guests leave their cards in the hall either when entering or leaving only at large garden parties.

DRESS. It is customary for women to wear light afternoon dresses.

Men wear summer business suits, yachting flannels, and straw hats, and even white duck trousers. Gloves are not worn.

The regulation frock coat and high hat is not worn, save by men from the city or at some extremely fashionable affair.

GUESTS. After leaving their outer garments in the dressing-rooms, the guests should pay their respects to the hostess, after which they are free to enjoy themselves as they please.

The usual length of stay is about half an hour or the whole afternoon.

While guests may arrive at their own convenient time, they would do well to remember that they have not the same freedom to come and go as at an afternoon reception.

Guests should take leave of the hostess unless she is very much engaged.

HOSTESS. The hostess wears afternoon dress, and usually one that is dainty and delicate-- suitable for a summer afternoon.

She receives on the lawn, shakes hands with each guest, and makes introductions when deemed essential.

She may, if she so desires, receive with some member of her family.

HOURS. These are from 3 to 7 P.M.

INVITATIONS. These are issued in the name of the hostess, and may be engraved or written. Sometimes the hostess writes on her card: GARDEN PARTY, JULY 17, FROM 4 TO 7, or she may use an AT HOME card, and in the lower left-hand corner write: GARDEN PARTY. The engraved card usually indicates an elaborate affair.

These invitations may be sent by mail or messenger.

It is a good plan to add to the invitations some information regarding the trains, or to enclose a time-table.

All such invitations should be promptly acknowledged or declined.

MEN. Men wear summer business suits, white ducks, or yachting flannels, A tennis suit would be permissible.

The regulation frock coat and high hat should be worn only by men from the city attending an affair in the country, or at some extremely fashionable affair.

Men should greet the hostess both on their arrival and departure.

Visiting-cards are left only at large garden parties.

WOMEN. Women wear light, delicate, afternoon dresses.

They should greet the hostess, both on their arrival and departure.

Visiting-cards are left only at large and formal outdoor affairs.

GERMANS. See COTILLIONS.

GIFTS.

AFTER HOUSE PARTY. While not necessary, a guest after a house party may send some trifle to the hostess as a token of pleasure and appreciation.

BEST MAN. After the groom selects the best man, the latter should send a gift to the bride, and may, if he wish, send it to the groom, a custom not yet clearly established.

CHRISTENING. A christening ceremony offers a good opportunity for the invited guests so wishing to send a gift to the baby. These should be sent a day or two before the ceremony, and, if of silver, should be suitably marked with the child's name, initials, or monogram.

ENGAGEMENT. If both families of the engaged couple are old acquaintances, the parents of the man may send a gift along with their greetings and congratulations.

WEDDING. See WEDDINGS--GIFTS.

GIFTS BETWEEN MEN AND WOMEN. Books, flowers, and other small articles of decoration are proper gifts to accept.

Sending valuable gifts of jewelry, or any other article, depends largely upon the relationships of the parties, and should not be done unless the sender is sure of its acceptance. Such gifts should not be accepted from mere acquaintances or friends.

It is bad form for a man to send expensive presents to a woman who may be compelled to return them.

GLOVES.

MEN. At the opera or theatre, if in full dress, gloves may be dispensed with, but they are worn with street dress. With formal evening dress, white kid gloves should be worn.

For afternoon dress, gloves should be of undressed kid, gray, tan, or brown. When calling, the glove of the right hand should be removed upon entering the drawing-room.

Gloves should not be worn at high teas.

MEN--AFTERNOON DRESS. Undressed kid gloves of a dark color are worn.

MEN-BALLS. Men should always wear gloves at all balls, in summer or winter, in town or city.

MEN-CALLING ON WOMEN. Gloves need not be removed at a formal or brief call.

MEN-DANCES. Gloves should be worn at formal dances, and should be put on before entering the room.

MEN-HIGH TEA. Men do not wear gloves.

MEN-MOURNING. Black or dark-colored gloves should be worn.

MEN--SHAKING HANDS. At weddings, operas, or dances, and on all very formal occasions, men wear gloves. In shaking hands with women on these occasions gloves should not be removed.

If a hostess wears gloves at any formal affair, a man wears his when he shakes hands with her.

A man with hands gloved should never shake hands with a woman without an apology for so doing, unless she likewise wears gloves. A sudden meeting, etc., may make a hand-shaking in gloves unavoidable. Unless the other party is also gloved, a man should say: "Please excuse my glove."

WOMEN. Gloves should always be worn on the street.

At dinners, or formal teas, women should remove their gloves at the table and place them in their laps.

At dinners and formal teas, when the women have retired to the drawing-room, they may resume their gloves or not, or follow the example of the hostess.

At informal teas or "At Homes" the hostess need not wear gloves.

BREAKFAST. Gloves should be removed at table.

DINNER. Women may remove their gloves at table, and it is not necessary to replace them. They should be laid in the lap. The hostess generally determines by her own actions whether the women should resume gloves or not.

MOURNING. Gloves may be of black kid, suede, or black silk. In the evening, black suede or glace, or white suede should be worn. White gloves with black stitching should not be worn in the evening.

BRIDE. See BRIDE--GLOVES.

GROOM. See GROOM--GLOVES.

USHERS. See USHERS--GLOVES.

GODFATHER. A man asked to be one of the sponsors at a christening ceremony should reply by a written note or by calling in person.

He should call immediately on the parents and send flowers to the mother, and express himself as pleased at the compliment.

He should send a present to the child, usually a piece of jewelry or some silver, and, if a wealthy relative, may deposit a sum of money to the child's credit, and present him with the bank-book.

He should also send with his present one of his calling cards, on which is written some appropriate sentiment.

It is his privilege, when the wine is about to be drunk after the ceremony, to first propose the health of the child and then the health of the mother.

The duties of the godfather at the ceremony consist of assenting to the vows.

GODMOTHER. A woman asked to be a sponsor at a christening should immediately accept or decline the invitation either by a written note or a call.

She should also call on the parents and send flowers to the mother, and express pleasure at the compliment paid to her.

It is always customary for the godmother to give the child a gift, such as a christening robe, a cradle, or some piece of silver. If the latter is sent, it should have the child's name on it. With the gift should be sent the sponsor's calling card, with some appropriate sentiment on it. It is customary to send the gift to the child itself.

GOLDEN WEDDINGS. Fifty years after the wedding-day comes the Golden Wedding. The invitations may bear the words: NO PRESENTS RECEIVED, and congratulations may be extended in accepting or declining the invitation. An entertainment is usually provided for.

The gifts are, appropriately, articles of gold, and this is a fitting occasion for giving fifty gold pieces of either, five, ten, or twenty dollar denomination. The invitations are appropriately engraved in gold, and the decorations golden in color.

GOVERNOR OF A STATE--HOW ADDRESSED. An official letter begins: Sir, and ends: I have the honor, sir, to remain your obedient servant.

A social letter begins: Dear Governor Wilson, and ends: Believe me, most sincerely yours.

The address on the envelope is: Governor John J. Wilson.

GRAPES AND PLUMS should be eaten one by one, and the pits allowed to fall noiselessly into the half-closed hand and then transferred to the plate.

GROOM. The groom selects his best man, usually an unmarried intimate friend, though a married man or widower is permissible. After consultation with the bride he calls upon the clergyman, the organist, the sexton, and invites the ushers.

When he is informed by his bride of the day selected for the wedding, he should ask her mother to accept the day agreed upon.

He may make what present he desires to the bride, and, if he also wishes, to the brides- maids. If any gifts are sent to the groom, they should bear his name or cipher.

He should furnish the bride's family with a list of names of persons to whom he desires to have invitations sent, designating his preference for those to be asked to the wedding breakfast or reception.

BEFORE CEREMONY. The day before the ceremony, or sooner, he gives into the safe- keeping of the best man the ring and the fee for the clergyman.

He also sends or hands the marriage license (if one is needed) to the officiating clergyman before the ceremony.

CHURCH, It is not customary for the groom to see his bride on the wedding-day till he meets her at the altar. The groom and the best man usually breakfast together on the wedding-day and arrive in ample time at the church.

Upon the arrival of the bride in the vestibule, the clergyman enters the chancel, followed by the groom and the best man. The groom then steps forward, and stands at the left of the clergyman, facing the audience. It is a good plan for both the groom and best man to leave their hats in the vestry, but if the groom has not done so, he gives his hat and gloves to the best man on the approach of the bride, and advances to meet her. He gives her his left arm, and together they stand before the clergyman.

At the proper moment he receives the ring from the best man and hands it to the bride. It is no longer in good form for him to kiss the bride after the ceremony, but after receiving the congratulations of the clergyman to give her his right arm, and together they lead the procession to the vestibule.

CLERGYMAN. While the bride selects the officiating clergyman, it is the place of the groom to call upon him in regard to the details, and to pay him the fee.

If the clergyman from any cause--as, living outside of the State--cannot legally perform the ceremony, a magistrate should be present to legalize the marriage, and should receive a fee.

DRESS-EVENING WEDDING. He wears full evening dress.

DRESS-MORNING OR AFTERNOON WEDDING. He wears afternoon dress, consisting of a double-breasted frock coat of dark material, waistcoat, single or double (preferably the latter), of same material, or more usually of some fancy material of late design. The trousers should be of light pattern, avoiding extremes. The linen should be white, and the tie white or light material, and the gloves of gray suede. These, with patent-leather shoes and a silk hat, complete the costume.

EXPENSES. He pays for the license fee, the organist's fee, and a fee to the sexton.

Nothing less than five dollars in gold, clean bills, or a check in a sealed envelope, or more, according to social position and financial income, should be the clergyman's fee. Should there be one or two additional clergymen, he pays a fee to each, the fee of the officiating clergyman being double that of the others.

He pays for the carriages of the ushers, the one for himself and the best man, and the one which takes away the married couple on their wedding trip.

He pays for the bouquet carried by the bride, and, if he wishes, for the bouquets carried by the bridesmaids. He also pays for the cuff-buttons or scarf-pins, and, if he wishes, for the gloves and neckties given to the ushers and the best man.

He pays for the wedding-ring--a plain gold one, with initials of bride and groom and date of marriage engraved thereon. He may also present some souvenirs to the bridesmaids.

He may give a farewell dinner a few evenings before the wedding to his best man, ushers, and a few intimate friends. He sits at the head of the table and the best man opposite, and on this occasion he may give the scarf-pins or cuff-buttons, also neckties and gloves, if he wishes, to the best man and ushers.

FAREWELL DINNER. See BACHELOR'S FAREWELL DINNER.

GLOVES. At a morning or afternoon wedding, the groom wears gray suede gloves.

At an evening wedding he wears white kid gloves.

WEDDING BREAKFAST. The bride and groom enter first, and are seated at the principal table.

WEDDING RECEPTION. The groom and his bride stand side by side and receive the congratulations of all present. The guests serve them refreshments.

See also BEST MAN. BRIDE. USHERS. All items under WEDDINGS.

GROOM'S FAMILY. See FAMILY OF GROOM.

GROOM'S FATHER. See FATHER OF GROOM.

GROOM'S MOTHER. See MOTHER OF GROOM.

GUESTS.

GUEST OF HONOR AT BALLS, if the ball is given in honor of some special person, he should be met on his arrival, introduced to the women of the reception committee, escorted to the seat prepared for him, and be attended to the whole evening by the management of the ball.

At the end of the ball, he should be escorted to his carriage.

LATE AT DINNERS. When a guest arrives late he should make a short and suitable apology to the hostess, and then take his seat as quickly and as quietly as possible.

The hostess shakes hands with the guest, but does not rise unless the guest is a woman.

The host should in either case rise and meet the guest, and assist him in finding his seat, and endeavor, by making the conversation general, to distract attention from the event.

For duties of guests, see other functions-- as, BALLS--GUESTS, CHRISTENINGS--GUESTS, etc.

HAND-SHAKING--INTRODUCTIONS. Women and men on being introduced may shake hands, but it is not good form. A polite bow, a smile, and friendly recognition is more correct. If an advance is made by either party, it should be immediately accepted.

HAT.

MEN--CALLING. When making a formal or brief call, the hat should be carried in the hand into the parlor.

In apologizing to a woman, opening a door, or rendering any service to a woman in public, or in answering a question, the hat should be raised.

When seeing a woman to her carriage, he should raise his hat upon closing the carriage door. When attentions are offered by another man to a woman whom he is escorting, a man raises his hat in acknowledgment of the courtesy and thanks the party.

In a street-car a man raises his hat when giving his seat to a woman.

On the railroad a man removes his hat in the parlor-car, but not in the day coach.

In an elevator a man should remove his hat in the presence of women.

In hotels where corridors are reserved and used as places of meeting and recreation by the guests, no hats should be worn. Standing uncovered when talking to a woman on the street is generally embarrassing to her, and it is better to make a polite bow and replace it after a few seconds.

MOURNING. A crape band around the hat should be worn--the width of the band being determined by the character of the bereavement.

HIGH TEA. This is an elaborate entertainment, and an elaborate menu is generally served.

CALLS. Calls should be made in person one week after the event.

GUESTS. Guests wear evening dress, and should not remain more than half an hour.

INVITATIONS. These are engraved, and the hour for the entertainment specified. They should be issued in the name of the hostess only, except in such cases when the entertainment is the occasion of a debut or another woman assists, in which event her name appears likewise.

The invitations should be promptly accepted or declined.

MEN. Full dress is worn, but men do not wear gloves.

WOMEN. Full dress is worn.

HOME WEDDINGS. Weddings at the homes of the brides vary much, according to the taste of the participants. The ushers, bridesmaids, best man, and maid of honor are generally dispensed with; but if present, their duties are the same as at a church wedding, with minor differences.

The clergyman stands in a large room decorated with flowers, facing the audience, with the groom beside him. The bride enters on the arm of her father, followed by the bridesmaids and ushers, and the ceremony proceeds as at a church, with the usual congratulations to the groom and best wishes to the bride.

Refreshments are served, either formal or informal. At an afternoon ceremony men wear the regulation afternoon dress, and if in the evening, the usual evening dress.

HONEYMOON, See WEDDING TRIP.

HONOR, SEAT OF. The seat of honor is at the right of the host.

HOST.

AFTERNOON TEAS. See AFTERNOON TEAS--HOST.

BACHELORS' DINNERS. See BACHELORS' DINNERS-- HOST.

BACHELORS' TEAS. See BACHELORS' TEAS--HOST.

BALLS. See BALLS--HOST.

DANCES. See DANCES (FORMAL)--HOST.

DINNERS. See DINNERS--HOST.

MATINEES. See MATINEES--HOST.

THEATRES. See THEATRE AND OPERA PARTIES GIVEN BY MEN.

HOSTESS.

INTRODUCTIONS. Introductions to the hostess at an "At Home" or reception by women assisting hostess, to those who have been invited to the entertainment by them, are not recognized thereafter unless by mutual consent.

The hostess receiving in her own home should offer her hand to all to whom she is introduced.

The hostess introduces her immediate family to all her guests. No formal permission is necessary.

In the case of one woman desiring an introduction to another, the hostess should be asked to bring this about.

INTRODUCTIONS BY CHAPERONES. At entertainments both the chaperone and her protege should enter together, and the chaperone should introduce her protege to the hostess.

WOMEN CALLING UPON. When calling formally upon a hostess, a woman should leave a card, whether the hostess was at home or not.

When a son enters society, his mother, when calling, can leave his cards for him, and invitations to entertainments will follow. If it is impossible for him to leave cards for himself she may continue to do so.

WOMEN LEAVING CARDS ON. When a mother leaves her daughter's card, it is for the hostess only.

HIGH TEAS. See HIGH TEAS--HOSTESS.

HOUSE PARTIES. See HOUSE PARTIES--HOSTESS.

LUNCHEONS. See LUNCHEONS--HOSTESS.

MATINEES. See MATINEES--HOSTESS.

SHAKING HANDS. See SHAKING HANDS--HOST.

WEDDINGS. See MOTHER OF BRIDE.

HOURS.

AFTERNOON TEAS. See AFTERNOON TEAS--HOURS.

BREAKFASTS. See BREAKFASTS--HOURS.

CALLS. See CALLS--HOURS.

DINNERS. See DINNERS--HOURS.

GARDEN PARTIES. See GARDEN PARTIES--HOURS.

LUNCHEONS. See LUNCHEONS--HOURS.

MUSICALES. See MUSICALES--HOURS.

RECEPTIONS. See RECEPTIONS--HOURS.

WEDDINGS. See WEDDINGS--HOURS.

HOUSE FUNERALS. See FUNERALS--HOUSE.

HOUSE PARTIES. These usually refer to a group of congenial persons, numbering from four to twenty-four, and visiting country homes, making a stay of a few days or a few weeks.

DRESS. The length of the visit and the nature of the house party determines the extent of wardrobe necessary. A guest should carry at least three changes of suits--one for the morning, one suitable for afternoon entertainments, picnics, etc., and the regulation evening dress.

GUEST. To be a welcome guest the visitor should accommodate himself as much as possible to the plans of his hostess and the ways of the home life.

A visitor should avoid the common mistake of refusing to make a choice when a choice is offered.

A guest should try to be congenial with the other guests, kind to the servants, and to be considerate of all others.

EXPENSES. The hostess should furnish transportation for both guests and baggage to and from the station.

Each guest should pay for all expenses incurred by him, and be especially careful, in the case of sickness or misfortune, that some items are not overlooked.

LETTER AFTER DEPARTURE. If the visit has been more than two days, the guest should write a short letter to the hostess, telling of the pleasure the visit gave them and their safe journey home.

A guest so desiring might send some trifle as a gift to the hostess.

TIPPING SERVANTS. Unless a hostess positively requests her guests not to tip, a guest, when leaving at the end of a visit at a private house, should remember the servants. The average American, from lack of a definite standard, too often errs on the side of giving too much.

Those giving personal service should be remembered, as well as those who render service-- as, the coachman and outside servants.

HOSTESS. While careful to provide entertainment for her guests, a hostess should be careful not to overentertain, and to allow each guest ample time in which to enjoy themselves any way they please. If an entertainment is planned for the afternoon, it is well to leave the mornings open, and VICE VERSA.

The success of the hostess depends on her making the guests feel free from care and ENNUI.

CARING POR THE SICK. In addition to the regular care of the guest's room and attention to his comfort and pleasure, a hostess should double her energies in case her guest is sick.

She is not called upon to pay for the expenses of telegrams, doctor's bills, medicines, etc., contracted by the guest. If a guest departed without attending to these matters, the hostess would have to pay for them.

GIVING FAREWELL, To VISITORS. A hostess should, in bidding farewell to her visitors, see that she does not overdo it.

While it is not strictly necessary that a hostess should accompany a guest to the depot, yet many still follow this rule, especially in the case of an unmarried woman, and are careful to see to all the details of checking baggage, etc.

In the case of a bachelor, such attention is not necessary.

A hostess conveys at her own expense both the guest and baggage to and from the station.

GREETING VISITORS. When an hour of arrival is specified in an invitation, the guest should be met at the station, especially an unmarried woman, by the hostess or host. In case of married couples or bachelors, a man servant may meet them.

In all cases the hostess should arrange for the conveyance of both the guests and their luggage.

A hostess accompanies a woman to the guest chamber, but sends a man servant with a bachelor to the latter's room.

INVITATIONS. These should state definitely when a visit is to begin and to end. It is also a good plan to allude in the invitation to any special amusement or entertainment.

These invitations should be answered promptly.

MEN--DRESS. A man should carry with him one business suit, evening clothes, and one outing suit suitable for afternoon entertainments --as, picnics, tennis, etc. This is almost indispensable, and more depends upon the nature of the entertainments and the length of the visit.

WOMEN--DRESS. A woman should take at least three changes of dress--one to travel in and wear in the morning, one for evening wear, and a third for afternoon picnics, outings, etc. The length of her visit and the nature of the entertainments and her individual taste determines how much she may increase this.

HOUSE OF REPRESENTATIVES, MEMBER OF. An official letter begins: SIR, and ends: I HAVE, SIR, THE HONOR TO REMAIN YOUR MOST OBEDIENT SERVANT.

A social letter begins: MY DEAR MR. WILSON and ends: I HAVE THE HONOR TO REMAIN MOST SINCERELY YOURS.

The address on the envelope is: HON. JOHN F. WILSON.

HUSBAND AND WIFE--CARDS, VISITING. See CARDS, VISITING-HUSBAND AND WIFE.

IN MEMORIAM CARDS. Printed or engraved notes, or special cards, can be used, and should be heavily bordered. Custom allows much diversity as to the contents of the card. Place and date of birth, residence, date of death, and any other information of interest to friends and relatives may be given.

INFANT'S CARDS. The full name of the child should be engraved, with date of birth in lower left-hand corner, enclosed in envelope with mother's card, and sent by mail. Such cards are generally held together with white ribbon.

INFORMAL AFTERNOON TEAS. These are the usual afternoon teas. By formal afternoon teas are meant those for which specially engraved cards have been issued, and at which all the arrangements are more elaborate.

See AFTERNOON TEAS.

INTERIOR, SECRETARY OF--HOW ADDRESSED. An official letter begins: Sir, and ends: I have, sir, the honor to remain your most obedient servant.

A social letter begins: My dear Mr. Wilson, and ends: I have the honor to remain most sincerely yours.

The address on the envelope is: Hon. John J. Wilson, Secretary Of The Interior.

INTRODUCTIONS. One should be careful in making introductions. It is easier to evade than to cause disagreeable complications. It is unpardonable to introduce one party to another after having been warned not to do so.

Forgetting a person's name when about to introduce is awkward, and when it does occur, one should apologize and ask name. If a person fails to hear the name, it is proper to inform the one to whom you are introduced and to say: "Pardon me, but I failed to hear your name." In making introductions one should distinctly pronounce the names.

Parents should not speak of or introduce their children as MISS ANNA, but simply MY DAUGHTER ANNA. Only before servants should they be spoken of as MISS ANNA.

Persons of celebrity should have introductions made to them. Men should always be introduced to women, the younger to an elder person, and unmarried persons to the married. Persons at an entertainment are introduced to the guest of the occasion.

Women and men on being introduced may shake hands, but it is not good form. A polite bow, a smile, and friendly recognition is more correct.

Those invited to an entertainment are on equal footing; it is therefore not necessary to introduce one to another. Conversation may be held without this formality, though introductions may take place if desired. When an introduction occurs, future recognition is not warranted. For this reason great care should be exercised at entertainments that only those who are congenial to each other should be brought together.

At small gatherings it is more kindly to introduce. When many are present, it is not customary to do so.

Introductions should not take place in a church or on the steps.

It is quite proper to introduce one group to another without formality at any outdoor function--athletic games, etc. Such introductions need not imply further acquaintance if undesirable.

DANCING. The man must be introduced to the woman, and he should ask her for the privilege of a dance.

ENTERTAINMENTS. Introductions are not absolutely required at musicales, teas, "At Homes," etc. One may converse with those nearest, but this does not warrant future recognition.

MEN. Men are introduced to women and single men to married men.

When introduced to a woman, a man should bow but not shake hands, and make some pleasant observations, and express pleasure at the introduction.

When introduced to another man, the man should shake hands.

Business introductions are immediate and personal, and are intended to bring men together without much formality. No formality is required in introducing one man to another on casual meeting.

It is well to avoid exaggerated expressions, as: "Delighted to meet you," or "Glad to know you." A simple "How do you do" is better.

A man introducing another to a woman should first ask her permission to do so. This gained, he introduces him with the remark: "Mr. Smith desires to be introduced to Miss Wilson."

A woman's permission should first be obtained by the party introducing. Very often off-hand introductions take place; but it is better to be more formal and careful, as indicated. If she evades or declines, a man should accept it without any show of feeling, and make it as easy for her as possible.

After an introduction at an entertainment, when a man meets the woman on the street, she should bow first if she desires to continue the acquaintance.

CHAPERONE. A man should never be introduced direct by card or letter to a young unmarried woman. If he desires to be introduced, the letter or card of introduction should be addressed to her chaperone or mother, who may then introduce him to the young woman if she deems it advisable.

At an entertainment a chaperone may ask a young man if he wishes to be introduced to the one under her care.

FORMULA. A good formula for men is: "Mr. Brown, may I present Mr. Clark?"

A man presenting a man friend to a woman should say: "Mr. Williams desires to be presented to Miss Wilson. Miss Wilson, allow me to introduce Mr. Williams. This is Mr. Williams, Miss Wilson."

The formality is sometimes waved, and the forms, "This is Mr. So and So, Miss Jones," "Mrs. Smith, Miss Jones," or "Allow me to present ----," are used when casual meetings occur.

PARTY INTRODUCED. After receiving call of party to whom you have been introduced, the visit should be returned. If AT HOME card was left, the call should be made only on the days specified; if an ordinary card, call at any time within three to ten days.

If the party introduced leaves town, he should send his card to his late host before leaving; upon his return, he should leave his card again.

PARTY INTRODUCING BY CARD--WOMEN. A note of explanation may be sent by party who brings about the introduction to the party to whom the introduction is made, giving such explanations as may be deemed advisable.

Two cards should be used--a person's own card and the card of the party being introduced, enclosed in envelope, and sent by mail or messenger. On the left corner over name of party introduced should be written: INTRODUCING MR. WILSON

PARTY INTRODUCING BY LETTER--WOMEN. Care should be exercised that the introduction is agreeable to all concerned.

RECEPTIONS. The man should express desire for an introduction.

WOMEN. Women calling and meeting others may be introduced to each other by the hostess. Upon such an occasion, when a meeting happens between women, conversation may take place between them without an introduction. It does not imply further acquaintance if not desired.

Extreme etiquette demands that no two women of the same locality be introduced to each other without the consent of both parties. The object of this is that, although the parties may be agreeable to the hostess, they may be objectionable to each other.

Women upon being introduced to each other may shake hands, but a slight inclination of the body, a smile, and an appropriate remark are more correct.

When entering a room where others are assembled, introducing a guest to more than one person at a time is unadvisable.

Men are introduced to women, single women to married women, and a young woman to an older one.

No woman should allow a man to be introduced to her unless her permission has been first obtained. The exception would be in the case of a very elderly man, or a celebrity, when the honor would be conferred upon her.

A married woman to whom a man is presented receives him with some pleasant remark. An unmarried one receives him with a pleasant smile and repeats his name.

Personal introduction is done by a third party introducing two persons to each other, provided it is agreeable to all concerned. Introductions should be made with extreme care and caution, and not at all unless one is well acquainted with both parties.

Outdoor Introductions--as, when meeting others, or at outdoor sports--need not be formal, but can be done haphazard. This does not imply further acquaintance if not desired.

FORMULA. A woman should introduce her husband to acquaintances as "My husband," and not "Mr."; to intimate friends as "Henry."

HOSTESS. Introductions to the hostess at an "At Home," or reception by women assisting hostess, of those who have been invited to the entertainment by them, are not recognized thereafter unless by mutual consent.

The hostess receiving in her own home should offer her hand to all to whom she is introduced.

The hostess introduces her immediate family to all her guests. No formal permission is necessary.

In the case of one woman desiring an introduction to another, the hostess should be asked to bring this about.

INTRODUCTION, LETTERS OF. The introduction of one person to another by letter is as follows: The party introducing writes the name of the party he introduces upon his own card, and above his name the words: Introducing Mr. Wilson (his friend's name). It is then placed in an envelope and addressed to the person to whom the introduction is to be made. On the lower left-hand corner of the envelope, Introducing Mr. Wilson, is written, and given to the bearer unsealed.

The party to whom a letter of introduction is given should send it by mail to the party they desire to be introduced to, enclosing their own card with address, and then await invitation to call.

This is preferable to calling in person, as it may not be agreeable or desirable for the party to open and begin such an acquaintance.

In business introduction, such formality may be set aside.

If a letter of introduction is personally delivered, the party presenting it should also enclose card.

If the party called upon is not at home, the letter or card should not be left, but sent by mail or messenger.

The one giving another a letter of introduction may write to the friend explaining why it is done, who and what the party is.

If a man sends a letter of introduction to a woman, she should acknowledge it, and, if she wishes, invite him to call.

PARTY RECEIVING--WOMEN. The party receiving cards of introduction should call in person upon woman introduced; if unable to do so, a letter should be sent, stating reasons of inability to be present. A member of the family may make the call instead. It should be done within three days.

If not agreeable to receive party for any reason, a card may be sent or left. No personal visit need be made.

INVALID'S CALLS. A woman unable to call from sickness may have her calls made for her by her sister, or daughter, or some female relative.

INVITATIONS. Care should be exercised in inviting new acquaintances to breakfast, luncheon, or dinner, unless there are some particular reasons why they will be especially agreeable to those invited.

All invitations should be sent by mail.

Verbal invitations should be avoided as much as possible, and if a verbal one is given, it should be followed immediately by one in writing.

ACCEPTING OR DECLINING. Invitations to all entertainments, when answers are expected, should be acknowledged by a written letter of acceptance or regret. The answer should be sent to the person or committee issuing the invitation.

Invitations to dinners, musicales, weddings, and breakfasts should be answered at once, and those to balls, dances, and receptions within one week.

Invitations to ordinary "At Homes," teas, or weddings, which do not include invitations to the wedding breakfast or reception, need no acknowledgment.

The invitations sent to a family--as, mother, or daughter, or several daughters-- may be answered by one person for all. But invitations sent to the men of the family should be answered by each man.

When it is found necessary to decline after accepting an invitation, a card should be sent the evening of the entertainment with an explanatory letter the day following.

BALLS. Invitations to balls or assemblies should be answered immediately, and if declined the ticket should be returned.

DANCING. While a woman may accept or decline any invitation to dance, it is considered a discourteous act to refuse one man and to accept thereafter from another an invitation to the same dance.

WEDDINGS. Such invitations should be answered at once, except when the invitation does not include an invitation to the wedding reception or breakfast, in which case no answer is needed.

ADDRESSING. When invitations are sent to a husband and wife and daughter, only one envelope is needed, the daughter's name appearing under her parents. Separate envelopes should be addressed to two daughters--as, Misses Wilson.

Separate envelopes should be addressed to each son.

MEN. If an invitation is sent to a man, he should answer it himself; but if sent to a man and wife, the latter may answer for both.

TO CALL WITH CHAPERONE'S PERMISSION. If permission is asked, and if agreeable, a chaperone should invite a man to call upon her and her protege.

Every effort should be made to call at the specified time.

TO CALL ON WOMEN. If a woman invites a man to call without specifying the time, it is equivalent to no invitation at all.

TO CALL ON WOMEN THROUGH LETTERS OF INTRODUCTION. If a man having a letter of introduction sends the same by mail to a woman, it should be acknowledged by a written invitation to call. If the person receiving the letter does not care to receive the party, a card is sent which ends the matter.

R. S. V. P. The use of these letters--standing for "Repondez, s'il vous plait" (Answer, if you please)--is decreasing. All invitations bearing these letters should be answered at once.

These may be used on invitations to ceremonious receptions, breakfasts, luncheons, dinners, and to meet a prominent person.

WIFE. When a husband and wife are invited to a dinner, and the former does not accept, the wife should also decline and give her reasons. The hostess can then invite the wife only, who may accept.

WOMEN. A young woman receiving an invitation to a man's supper, tea, or dinner, may accept, if she has the consent of her mother or chaperone, and is assured that a chaperone will be present.

WOMEN--THEATRE. Women receiving an invitation from a man for the theatre should have the consent of mother or chaperone, and when they accept, may, with propriety, request their escort not to provide a carriage unless full dress on their part is requested.

AFTERNOON TEAS. See AFTERNOON TEAS--INVITATIONS. AFTERNOON TEAS (FORMAL)--INVITATIONS.

AT HOMES. See AT HOMES--INVITATIONS.

BACHELORS' DINNERS. See BACHELORS' DINNERS--INVITATIONS.

BACHELORS' TEAS. See BACHELORS' TEAS--INVITATIONS.

BALLS. See BALLS--INVITATIONS.

BREAKFASTS. See BREAKFASTS--INVITATIONS.

BRIDE. See BRIDE--INVITATIONS.

CHRISTENINGS. See CHRISTENINGS--INVITATIONS.

COTILLIONS. See COTILLIONS--INVITATIONS. See COTILLIONS BY SUBSCRIPTIONS--INVITATIONS.

MUSICALES. See MUSICALES--INVITATIONS.

PALL-BEARERS. See PALL-BEARERS--INVITATIONS.

PARTIES. See PARTIES--INVITATIONS.

TELEPHONE. See TELEPHONE INVITATIONS.

THEATRE. See THEATRE AND OPERA PARTIES GIVEN BY MEN--INVITATIONS.

VERBAL. See VERBAL INVITATIONS.

IVORY WEDDING. This is the thirtieth wedding anniversary, and is not usually celebrated. If, however, it is done, the invitations may bear the words: NO PRESENTS RECEIVED, and in accepting or declining the invitation congratulations may be extended. Any article of ivory is appropriate as a gift. An entertainment is usually provided.

JEWELRY--MEN. Jewelry, except the very plainest, should not be worn, and in general the less the better. A display of diamonds and fancy jewelry betrays the poor taste of the wearer.

A man wearing the pins and badges of secret societies should see that they are small and unobtrusive, for in jewelry, as in all matters of dress, quality rather than quantity is to be desired.

JR. When the son is named after the father, he adds Jr. to his name. Upon the death of the father he omits it. This abbreviation is sometimes added to a woman's name on her card when her husband has the same name as his father, and it is necessary to distinguish between the cards of the daughter-in-law and the mother-in-law.

If the mother-in-law should become a widow and wish to retain the husband's baptismal name, she should add Sr., while her daughter would erase Jr.

If both become widows, and wish to retain their husband's Christian names, the daughter-in-law should add Jr.

JUSTICE OF THE UNITED STATES SUPREME COURT--HOW ADDRESSED. An official letter begins: Sir, and ends: I have, sir, the honor to remain your most obedient servant.

A social letter begins: Dear Justice Wilson, and ends: Believe me, most sincerely yours.

The address on the envelope is: Mr. Justice John J. Wilson.

KING OF ENGLAND--HOW ADDRESSED. An official letter begins: Sir, may it please your Majesty, and ends: I have the honor to remain your Majesty's most obedient servant.

A social letter begins: Dear Sir, and ends: I have the honor to remain your Majesty's most obedient servant.

The address on the envelope is: To His Most Gracious Majesty, King Edward.

KISS, WEDDING. The kiss in the wedding ceremony is being done away with, especially at church weddings. Only the bride's parents and her most intimate friends should kiss her, and for others to do so is no longer good form.

KNIFE AND FORK. The knife is always held in the right hand, and is only used for cutting the food. The fork is used not only in eating fish, meat, vegetables, and made dishes, but also ices, frozen puddings, melons, salads, oysters, clams, lobsters, and terrapin.

The knife should never be used to carry food to the mouth.

See also SPOON.

KNIGHT--HOW ADDRESSED. An official letter begins: Sir, and ends: I have the honor to remain, sir, your obedient servant.

A social letter begins: Dear Sir John Wilson, and ends: Believe me, dear Sir John, faithfully yours.

The address on the envelope is: To Sir John Wilson.

WIFE OF. See Wife of Knight.

LAUNDRESS--TIPS. Guests at the end of a house party do not tip the laundress unless she has done special work for them.

LEATHER WEDDING. This is the twelfth anniversary of the wedding-day, and is not usually observed. If, however, it is observed, the invitations may bear the words: No presents received, and congratulations may be extended in its acceptance or declination. Any article of leather would be an appropriate gift. An entertainment usually follows.

LETTERS.

ADDRESSING. See ADDRESSING AND SIGNING LETTERS, and also under title of person addressed --as, GOVERNOR, MAYOR, etc.

WRITTEN AFTER HOUSE PARTIES. If the visit has been more than two days in length, a guest should write to the hostess a short letter, telling of his pleasant visit and safe journey home.

CONCLUSION OF. See CONCLUSION OF A LETTER.

OF CONDOLENCE. See CONDOLENCE, LETTERS OF.

OF INTRODUCTION. See INTRODUCTION, LETTERS OF.

LETTUCE leaves should not be cut, but folded up with a fork, and then lifted to the mouth. In the event of these being too large for this treatment, they should be broken into suitable pieces with the fork.

LICENSE, MARRIAGE. A license, when required by State law, should be obtained by the groom and handed to the officiating clergyman the day before the ceremony. Usually a small fee is charged, and the details, when entered upon the clerk's records, are open to public inspection. The day need not be named, and until the marriage is solemnized the license has no binding effect.

LUNCHEONS. Usually only women are invited to these entertainments. Oddities, such as pink, blue, and yellow luncheons, are not in good taste. They should be as simple as possible.

Informal luncheons are the same as informal breakfasts. A more formal luncheon is proper when introducing a special guest.

Small tables are used, and diagrams of their arrangement are placed in the dressing-room, designating the places of the guests.

CALLS. Calls should be made a week after entertainment.

WOMEN. Women dress in visiting toilettes and wear their bonnets, laying aside their wraps in the dressing-room. Gloves should be removed at table.

After coffee, the guests should take their leave, making some gracious remark to the hostess.

Calls should be made a week after the entertainment.

GIVEN BY BACHELORS. See Bachelors' Luncheons.

GUESTS. Only women, as a rule, attend luncheons. For further details, see LUNCHEONS--WOMEN.

HOSTESS. Introductions take place in the parlor. At the appointed hour the hostess leads the way to the drawing-room, followed by the guests.

The hostess and principal guest should sit at one of the centre-tables. Between the courses the hostess and two of the women seated with her rise and change seats with others. This may be done by others also if they desire. They take their napkins with them.

HOURS. The hour is from 1 to 2 P.M.

INTRODUCTIONS. Introductions take place in the parlor.

INVITATIONS. Cards are engraved, and sent two weeks in advance.

MEN--LEAVING CARDS. If men are invited, they should, after a luncheon, leave a card for host and hostess, whether the invitation was accepted or not; or it may be sent by mail or messenger, with an apology for so doing.

MAIDS--TIPS. It is customary for guests leaving after a visit at a private house to remember the maid who has taken care of the room by giving her a reasonable tip. A woman should give more for extra attention.

MAID OF HONOR. This important person is selected by the bride, and acts for her in all details, being virtually mistress of ceremonies and filling a position requiring administrative ability and tact. She acts in the same capacity as the best man does for the groom.

She is invited, of course, to the dinner given by the bride to the bridesmaids.

She fulfils whatever duties the bride has been unable, from press of time, to attend to --as, making calls, etc.

CHURCH. She goes to the church with one of the parents of the bride, and meets the bride and the bridesmaids in the vestibule. In the procession she follows behind the bridesmaids, and precedes the flower girl, if there is one-- otherwise the bride. On their arrival at the altar she takes her place by the side of the bride, and is ready at the plighting of the troth to take the bride's glove and bouquet, and returns them to her at the end of the ceremony.

After the congratulations of the clergyman, she parts the bridal veil, arranges the bride's train, and follows the bride down the aisle to the vestibule.

Here, after giving her best wishes to the bride, she takes her carriage to the bride's house to take part in the reception or breakfast.

DAY OF WEDDING. She should be at the house of the bride on the morning of the wedding-day to assist the bride's mother, to see that the trousseau is all ready and packed, that the bridesmaids are on time, and to attend to the many details liable to arise.

DRESS. Her dress should be some delicate color other than white, so as not to detract from the bride, and should be subdued in comparison. It may be, and usually is, more elegant in quality than that of the bridesmaids.

WEDDING BREAKFAST. The best man escorts the maid of honor, and they are usually seated at the bridal table.

WEDDING RECEPTION. She stands next the bride to receive with her, and also retires with her to assist the latter in exchanging her wedding dress for the traveling-dress.

It is her privilege to cast a slipper at the carriage which takes away the married couple, and her duty to prepare packages of rice, which are given to the guests to be thrown after the married couple as they leave the house.

MAIL, INVITATIONS SENT BY. All invitations should be sent by mail and verbal ones avoided.

MAIL OR MESSENGER, SENDING CARDS BY. See CARDS, VISITING--SENDING BY MAIL OR MESSENGER.

MAN SERVANTS--TIPS. It is customary for a man, at the end of a house party, to give to the man servant who has acted as his valet a suitable tip.

MARCHIONESS-HOW ADDRESSED. An official letter begins: Madam, and ends: I have the honor to remain your Ladyship's most obedient servant.

The address on the envelope is: To the Most Noble the Marchioness of Kent.

A social letter begins: Dear Lady Kent, and ends: Believe me, dear Lady Kent, very sincerely yours.

The address on the envelope is: To the Marchioness of Kent.

MARCHIONESS, DOWAGER--HOW ADDRESSED. An official letter begins:

Madam, and ends: I have the honor to remain your Ladyship's most obedient servant.

A social letter begins: Dear Lady Kent, and ends: Believe me, dear Lady Kent, very sincerely yours.

The address on the envelope in both cases is: To the Dowager Marchioness of Kent, or To Mary, Marchioness of Kent.

MARQUIS--HOW ADDRESSED. An official letter begins: My Lord Marquis, and ends: I have the honor to be your Lordship's obedient servant.

The address on the envelope is: To the Most Noble the Marquis of Kent.

A social letter begins: Dear Lord Kent and ends: Believe me, Lord Kent, very sincerely yours.

The address on the envelope is: To the Marquis of Kent.

MARQUIS.

DAUGHTER OF. See DAUGHTER OF MARQUIS.

WIFE OF YOUNGER SON OF. See WIFE OF YOUNGER SON OF MARQUIS.

YOUNGER SON OF. See SON (YOUNGER) OF MARQUIS.

MARKING WEDDING PRESENTS. While it is not strictly necessary that wedding presents be marked, yet it is customary, and they should always be marked with the bride's maiden name, unless specially intended for the groom's individual use.

MATINEES. Proper music should be provided.

The refreshment-room should be within easy reach. Light dainties should be served occasionally to those not caring to go to the refreshment-room.

DRESS. If after six o'clock, evening dress should be worn; otherwise, afternoon dress.

HOST. The head of the house need not be present.

HOSTESS. The hostess and those assisting her should not dance, unless all her guests are provided with partners or are otherwise entertained.

INVITATIONS. These may be written or engraved, with Dancing and the hour for beginning in the lower left-hand corner. They should be sent two weeks in advance, and should be promptly answered.

MEN. Gloves should be worn when dancing. See also BALLS. COTILLIONS. DANCES. DANCING.

MAYOR OF A CITY--HOW ADDRESSED. An official letter begins: Sir, or Your Honor, and ends: I have the honor, sir, to remain your obedient servant.

A social letter begins: My dear Mayor Wilson, or, Dear Mr. Wilson, and ends: Believe me, most sincerely yours.

The address on the envelope is: His Honor, the Mayor of Kent, John J. Wilson.

MEN.

ADDRESSING ENVELOPES. See ADDRESSING ENVELOPES--MEN.

AFTERNOON DRESS. See AFTERNOON DRESS--MEN.

AFTERNOON TEAS. See AFTERNOON TEAS--MEN.

SHAKING HANDS. See SHAKING HANDS--MEN.

STATIONERY. See STATIONERY--MEN.

STREET-CARS. See STREET-CARS--MEN.

STREET ETIQUETTE. See STREET ETIQUETTE--MEN.

THEATRE PARTIES. See THEATRE PARTIES--MEN.

TITLES. See TITLES--MEN.

TRAVELING. See TRAVELING--MEN.

WEDDINGS. See WEDDINGS--MEN.

MESSENGER, SENDING CARDS BY. See CARDS, VISITING-- SENDING BY MAIL OR MESSENGER.

MINISTER (PROTESTANT)-HOW ADDRESSED, An official letter begins: Reverend Dear Sir, and ends: I remain sincerely yours.

A social letter begins: Dear Mr. Wilson, and ends: I beg to remain sincerely yours.

The address on the envelope is: The Reverend John J. Wilson. but if the clergyman holds the degree of D.D. (Doctor of Divinity), the address may be: The Reverend John J. Wilson, D.D., or Reverend Dr. John J. Wilson.

MINISTER. See CLERGYMAN.

MISS. This is the prefix both in conversation, correspondence, and on the visiting-card of the eldest daughter, the next daughter being known as Miss

Annie Smith; but on the death or marriage of the eldest daughter, she becomes Miss Smith.

MONOGRAMS. If men and women wish, these may be stamped in the latest colors on their stationery. When the address is stamped, it is not customary to stamp the monogram.

The latest fashion in the style of monograms require that they should be the size of a ten-cent piece.

All individual eccentricities of facsimiles of handwriting, etc., should be avoided.

It is not customary to have the monogram on the flap of the envelope.

If sealing-wax is used, it should be of some dull color.

MORNING DRESS. MEN. Morning costume consists of a dark frock coat, with vest and light trousers. This can be worn at any entertainment occurring in the daytime--as, weddings, luncheons, receptions of all kinds, matinees, or ceremonious visits.

Anything worn is admissible in morning dress, a business suit, cutaway, sack suit, hats or caps, and undressed kid gloves of a dark color.

At out-of-town resorts, golf, wheeling, and yachting costumes suitable for outdoor sport may be worn in the morning.

It is considered the correct thing for a man to tie his own tie instead of buying them ready made.

See also AFTERNOON DRESS--MEN. EVENING DRESS--MEN.

MOTHER. A mother should receive an invitation for any function to which her daughters are invited, and should go and return with them.

DEBUTS. The mother and the elder unmarried daughter, prior to the debut, calls formally upon those who are to be invited. She stands at her daughter's side to receive the congratulations of the guests, and at a dance she selects the first partner to dance with the debutante, and at the dinner or supper is escorted by the most distinguished man. See also CHAPERONE.

MOTHER OF BRIDE. At the wedding reception she is escorted by the father of the groom, and receives with the married couple.

At the wedding breakfast she is escorted by the father of the groom.

MOTHER OF GROOM. At the wedding reception she receives with the married couple.

At the wedding breakfast she is taken in by the father of the bride, following after the ushers and the maids of honor.

MOURNING. Those in mourning for parent, child, brother, or husband should not be seen at any public function or private entertainment before six months have passed.

CARDS. These are the same size as visiting-cards. A black border is used, the width to be regulated by the relationship to the deceased relative.

They should be sent to indicate temporary retirement from and re-entrance into society.

Within a month after death in a family friends should leave cards. The persons receiving the same should acknowledge the remembrance and sympathy when they are ready to resume their social functions. This may be done by letter or card.

MEN. Mourning cards are the same size as visiting-cards, and a black border is used, the width to be regulated by the relationship of deceased relative.

WOMEN. Mourning cards should be sent, to indicate temporary retirement from society. Later cards should be sent, to indicate return to society.

CHILDREN. Children under twelve need not be dressed in mourning, though they often are. Only the lightest material should be used. Girls of more advanced age do not wear veils, but crape may be worn in hat or dress, according to taste.

For parent, brother, or sister, mourning is worn for about one year.

MEN. Men wear mourning one year for loss of wife.

A crape band should be worn around the hat, its width being determined by the nearness of the relative mourned for. It is usually removed after eight months.

A widower wears mourning for one year, or, if he wishes, eighteen months, and for a brother, sister, parent, or a child, from six months to a year, as he desires. For the loss of other relatives, duration of mourning is generally regulated by the members of the family.

The wearing of a black band on the coat sleeve in token of half-mourning is an English custom, and is somewhat practised in this country.

STATIONERY-MEN. A widower uses a black border about one-third of an inch on his stationery, and this at intervals is diminished.

All stamping should be done in black.

WOMEN. A widow's stationery should be heavily bordered, and is continued as long as she is in deep mourning. This is gradually decreased, in accordance with her change of mourning.

All embossing or stamping should be done in black.

WEDDINGS. Mourning should never be worn at a wedding, but it should be laid aside temporarily, the wearer appearing in purple.

WIDOWS. A widow should wear crape with a bonnet having a small border of white. The veil should be long, and worn over the face for three months, after which a shorter veil may be worn for a year, and then the face may be exposed. After six months white and lilac may be used, and colors resumed after two years.

WOMEN. The mourning dress of a woman for parent, sister, brother, or child is the same as that worn by a widow, save the white bonnet ruche--the unmistakable mark of a widow.

For parents and children, deepest mourning is worn at least one year, and then the change is gradually made by the addition of lighter material or half-mourning.

For other members of the family--as, aunts, uncles, grandparents, cousins, etc.--black clothes should be worn, but not heavy mourning.

Complimentary mourning is worn for three months; this does not necessitate crape and veil, but any black material can be used.

WOMEN, FOR CHILDREN. For a child, mourning is usually worn for six months, thereafter substituting black and white.

FOR BROTHER AND SISTER, ETC. Mourning for a brother or sister, step-parents, or grandparents is the same as for parents, but the time is shorter, generally about six months. For an aunt, uncle, or cousin the time is three months.

FOR FIANCE. In the event of the death of a woman's betrothed shortly before the date of the wedding, she may wear black for a short period or full mourning for a year.

FOR HUSBANDS. Mourning cards are sent out, to indicate that they are not making or receiving calls.

Mourning is generally worn for two years, and sometimes much longer. Woolen material of the deepest black and crape should be worn during the first year.

When out-of-doors a crape veil should be worn for a year, or at least three months, covering the face, or, if preferred, the veil may be thrown over the shoulder, and a small one of tulle, or other suitable material, edged with crape, worn over the face.

A crape bonnet should be worn, and a very small white ruche may be added if desired.

After the first year a gradual change to lighter mourning may be made by discarding the widow's cap and shortening the veil. Dull silks are used in place of crape, according to taste. In warm weather lighter materials can be worn-- as, pique, nun's veiling, or white lawn.

Black furs and sealskin may be worn. Precious stones, such as diamonds and pearls, may be used if mounted in black enamel. Gold jewelry should not be used. A woman should avoid all pretensions to excessive styles.

FOR HUSBAND'S RELATIVES. A married woman wears mourning for her husband's immediate relatives.

FOR PARENTS AND GRANDCHILDREN. Mourning for these persons is generally worn for one year. During the first six months, black material trimmed with crape is used, and also a deep veil, which is thrown over the back of the head and not worn over the face, as for a husband. After this period the mourning may be lightened, according to taste.

See also DEATH IN THE FAMILY. FUNERALS.

MR. AND MRS. CARDS (VISITING). These cards are not generally used for ceremonious calls after the first series of return calls made by the bride.

If the husband is unable, the first year after marriage, to make formal calls, his wife uses the Mr. and Mrs. cards, and such is accepted as a call from him. But after one year she should leave their separate cards.

These are used on formal occasions-as, returning a first call, condolence, congratulations, or P. P. C.--when both the husband and wife are represented.

When they are used the first year after marriage, they should have the address in right-hand corner and reception days in lower left-hand corner.

The card should read: Mr. and Mrs. Thomas Wren Wilson

MUSIC.

WEDDINGS. The organist and the music are usually selected by the bride. Before her arrival, the organist plays some bright selection; but on her entering the church and passing up the aisle, he plays the wedding march.

AFTBRNOON TEAS (FORMAL). Music is always appropriate on these occasions.

MUSICALES.

DRESS. The rule would be that at an afternoon affair afternoon dress would be worn, and evening dress at an evening affair.

HOURS. For an afternoon musicale, the hours are usually from four to six. For an elaborate evening drawing-room concert, any hour may be selected.

INVITATIONS. These are sent out two weeks before the event. If entertainment is in the evening, they should be issued by husband and wife. If given in honor of a prominent person at any hour whatever, the cards should be engraved, and in either case the word Music should appear in the lower left- hand corner.

These should be acknowledged at once by a letter of acceptance or regret.

NAPKINS, when in use, are laid on the lap, and, when finished with, are not folded up unless one is a guest for a few days; on all other occasions they are left unfolded. A good plan is to follow the example of the hostess.

When fruit is brought on, a small fruit napkin is placed across the knee or held in the right hand, with which to hold the fruit, and when it is no longer needed, it should be laid beside the plate.

NAVY, SECRETARY OF--HOW ADDRESSED. An official letter begins: Sir, and ends: I have, sir, the honor to remain your most obedient servant.

A social letter begins: My dear Mr. Wilson, and ends: I have the honor to remain most sincerely yours.

The address on the envelope is: Hon. John J. Wilson, Secretary of the Navy.

NEW ACQUAINTANCES.

WOMEN. New acquaintances should not be invited to entertainments unless agreeable to all concerned.

An entertainment can be given to meet new acquaintances if there be some special reason for so doing.

Elderly persons and professional people can send their cards to younger persons if they wish to continue acquaintance.

NEWCOMERS.

BALL INVITATIONS. It is allowable for a new- comer wishing to give a ball to borrow the visiting list of some friend; but she should enclose in each invitation a calling card of this friend, so that the invited ones may know that the friend is acting as a sponsor.

DUTY OF. No effort should be made to obtain recognition of older residents.

Visits from neighbors should be returned within a week. If from any reason a newcomer is unable to call, a note stating the reason should be sent.

If visit of neighbor's male relative is desired, a woman may send him a written or verbal invitation; but if visit is not desired, no notice is taken of his card, in the event of one having been left.

RESIDENTS' DUTY TO MEN. When calling, kinswoman leaves cards of all the male members of family who are in society. If these cards left by kinswoman are not followed by an invitation to call, it is presumed that the acquaintance is not desired. Men can not call upon women of the family of new resident, unless invited to do so by either verbal or written message.

RESIDENTS' DUTY TO WOMEN. The newcomer receives the first call from the older resident, which should be made within a reasonable time. Women making the first call, leave their own card and those of the male members of the family.

It is unnecessary to be introduced in the absence of letters of introduction. Visits should be of short duration.

OLIVES are eaten with the fingers.

OPERA. See THEATRE.

ORANGES, served in divided sections, sweetened, and the seeds removed, should be eaten with the fork. If served whole, cut into suitable portions. Remove seed and skin.

ORGANIST AT WEDDINGS. The organist is selected by the bride, but the fee is paid by the groom.

OVERCOAT--MEN CALLING ON WOMEN. When making a formal or brief call, the overcoat should be left in the hall.

P. P. C. CARDS (VISITING). These letters--standing for Pour prendre conge (To take leave)--are written in the lower left-hand corner of the visiting-card. These cards are used as a formal farewell to such friends and acquaintances whose friendship it is desired to continue.

They may be left in person, or sent upon departure from city or winter or summer resort. They are rarely used in brief visits, and should only be used at the close of a season.

Care should be exercised in sending them, as an oversight in so doing may cause the loss of good friends.

PAGES AT WEDDINGS. At the wedding, if pages are present, they are usually dressed in satin court costumes, and carry the bride's train.

PALL-BEARERS. It is not good taste to ask relatives to be pall-bearers. The usual number is six to eight elderly men for elderly person, and of young men for a young man. Six young women in white would be a suitable number to act as pall-bearers for a young woman.

Pall-bearers should be asked either by note or by a representative of the head of the family of the deceased.

The pall-bearers assemble at the house at the appointed hour, and there take the carriages reserved for them. They disperse after the church service.

Except in the case of young women, carriages are not sent to bring pall-bearers to the house.

CALLS. After accepting an invitation to act as a pall-bearer, a man should call at the house of the bereaved and leave his card.

A few days after the funeral he should call again and leave his card. If he wishes, he may simply ask at the door after the women of the family.

DRESS. The pall-bearers wear black frock coat, trousers, and waistcoat, a black silk hat with a mourning band, black shoes, and black kid gloves. The linen should be white

FLOWERS. Unless there has been a request not to send flowers, a pall-bearer may do so after his first call.

If he wishes, a few days after the funeral he may send flowers to the women of the family with his card, on which should be written: With the compliments of -----.

INVITATIONS. The invitation should be promptly accepted or declined, and if accepted only illness or unavoidable absence from the city would excuse a man from attending.

PAPER WEDDING. The first wedding anniversary is called the paper wedding, and is not usually celebrated. If, however, it is celebrated, the invitations may bear the words: No presents received. Congratulations should be extended in accepting or declining the invitations. Any article of paper would be an appropriate gift. An entertainment should follow.

PARTIES. These are less formal than balls.

They generally begin at nine or nine-thirty, with dancing at ten-thirty or eleven. The supper precedes the dancing. Those who do not take part in the dancing may leave before it begins.

INVITATIONS. These are engraved, giving hour for beginning in lower left-hand corner, and should be sent two weeks in advance. One envelope only need be used. They should be answered promptly.

PATRONESSES. It is customary for the management of any institution giving a public ball to formally invite six, eight, or more married women to act as patronesses, and for their names to appear on the invitations. If badges are worn, each patroness is sent one or given one at the ball-room.

The patronesses, after being welcomed at the ball by the management committees, take their places, ready to receive the guests.

The Committee of Arrangements should look after the patronesses, introduce distinguished guests to them, escort them to supper and finally to their carriages.

See also COTILLIONS BY SUBSCRIPTIONS-- PATRONESSES. DANCES.

PEACHES should be quartered and the quarters peeled, then taken up by the fingers and eaten.

PEAS are eaten with a fork.

PLUMS AND GRAPES should be eaten one by one, and the pits allowed to fall noiselessly into the half-closed hand and then transferred to the plate.

POSTAL CARDS. It is wise to restrict the use of postals to impersonal communications; but if they must be used, the message should be brief with an apology for its use. It is a good plan in addition to omit the usual My dear, and to sign with the initials only and the full surname.

POSTPONING DINNERS See CANCELING DINNERS.

POSTPONING WEDDINGS. See WEDDINGS--INVITATIONS RECALLED.

PRECEDENCE.

DINNERS. See DINNERS--PRECEDENCE.

FUNERALS. See FUNERALS--PRECEDENCE.

THEATRE. See THEATRE--PRECEDENCE.

PRESENTS. See GIFTS.

PRESIDENT--HOW ADDRESSED. An official letter begins: Sir, and ends: I have the honor to remain your most obedient servant.

A social letter begins: My dear Mr. President, and ends: I have the honor to remain most sincerely yours.

The address on the envelope is: President John Wilson.

PRINCE, ROYAL--HOW ADDRESSED. An official letter begins: Sir, may it please your Royal Highness, and ends: I have the honor to remain, sir, your Royal Highness' humble servant.

A social letter begins: Dear Sir, and ends: Your Royal Highness' most obedient servant.

The address on the envelope is: To His Royal Highness, the Prince of Wales.

PRINCESS, 'ROYAL-HOW ADDRESSED. An official letter begins: Madam, may it please your Royal Highness, and ends: Your Royal Highness' most obedient servant.

A social letter begins: Dear Madam, and ends: Your Royal Highness' most obedient servant.

The address on the envelope is: To Her Royal Highness, the Princess of Wales.

PRIVATE WEDDINGS. These are attended only by intimate friends and members of the family, and vary but little from home weddings.

If the family is in mourning the cards are issued with the name of bride and groom and new address, together with card having bride's maiden name, and the announcement cards are sent after the ceremony.

Afternoon dress should be worn at an afternoon wedding, and evening dress at an evening wedding.

PROPOSALS OF MARRIAGE. The time, manner, and details of proposals of marriage are appropriately left to the good taste and judgment of the groom. If the proposal is rejected, good taste, womanly refinement, and courteous consideration demand that it be kept an inviolate secret, and any such breach of confidence may be rightly deemed the act of a woman without taste or tact, and unworthy of respect.

Proposals by women, while permissible, are not customary.

PUBLIC BALLS, By public balls are meant county and charity balls, and balls given by social institutions where dancing is the main feature. These public balls differ from private ones in that all the duties of the hostess fall upon some committees.

These committees would follow the same rules as laid down for a hostess-- issuing engraved invitations from fourteen to seventeen days in advance, engaging a caterer, etc.

The etiquette for a public ball is the same as for a private one, save that guests arrive and depart when they please without taking leave of those who receive, and men wishing introductions apply for them to the Floor or Reception Committee.

At the cloak-rooms a small fee is paid to the attendant.

SEE ALSO all entries under Balls.

BADGES. It is customary for the men and women on the committees to wear on the left side of the breast ornamental and embroidered badges, with the official position designated on it.

COMMITTEE. The committee at a public ball takes the place of the hostess, filling all her duties and offices.

PATRONESSES. It is customary for the management formally to invite six, eight, or more married women to act as patronesses of the ball, and for their names to appear on the invitations. If badges are prepared for the patronesses, one is sent to each patroness or handed to her on the evening of the dance.

The patronesses should be welcomed at the ball by the management, and they then take their position ready to receive the guests.

The management should look after the patronesses, to see that they are taken into supper, to introduce prominent guests to them, and, finally, to escort the patronesses to their carriages.

PUBLIC PLACES. SEE ALSO ELEVATORS. RESTAURANTS, STREET-CARS. STREET ETIQUETTE.

R. S. V. P. The use of these letters-standing for Repondez, s'il vous plait (Answer, if you please)-is decreasing. All invitations to which acceptances are expected should be answered at once. If preferred, however, the above abbreviations may be used on the following: invitations to ceremonious receptions, breakfasts, luncheons, dinners, and to meet a prominent person.

RAILROAD-MEN. A man should remove his hat in a parlor-car, but not in a day coach.

RECALLING WEDDING INVITATIONS. When from some good reason a wedding has to be canceled or postponed, the parents of the bride should send, as soon as possible, printed notices, giving reasons to all the guests.

RECEPTIONS. Reception days are placed in the lower left-hand corner of visiting-cards-as, UNTIL LENT, or, In JANUARY-and may be either engraved or written.

Daughters have no reception day of their own, but receive on their mother's reception day.

The etiquette at receptions is the same as at afternoon teas.

SEE ALSO AFTERNOON TEAS. AT HOMES.

HOURS. Afternoon receptions are held from 4 to 7 P.M.

Evening receptions are held from 9 to 11 P.M.

INVITATIONS, ACCEPTING OR DECLINING. These should be acknowledged within a week, either by a letter accepting, or declining with regret.

INTRODUCTIONS. The man should seek an introduction to any woman he wants to meet.

The hostess makes what introductions she deems proper.

DRESS. For an afternoon reception guests should wear afternoon dress, and for an evening reception evening dress.

AFTERNOON, GIVEN BY BACHELORS. See BACHELORS' TEAS.

EVENING. The etiquette is the same as for an afternoon tea (formal), save that no cards are left by the guests, and that the guests should wear evening dress.

See also AFTERNOON TEAS (FORMAL).

WEDDING. See WEDDING RECEPTIONS.

REFRESHMENTS.

WEDDING RECEPTIONS. The refreshments are placed on tables, and the guests help themselves or are helped by the bridesmaids. The groom and bride are waited upon by the guests.

REGISTER, SIGNING OF. This is sometimes done by the bride and the groom. This takes place in the vestry, and the best man signs as chief witness and some of the guests as witnesses.

REHEARSALS, WEDDING. Rehearsals should be held even for a quiet home wedding, and at a sufficiently early date to insure the presence of all who are to participate.

REPORTERS AT WEDDINGS. If such is the wish of the family of the bride, the best man attends to the reporters, and furnishes them with the names of groom, bride, relatives, friends, description of gowns, and other suitable details.

RESIDENCE, CHANGE OF--WOMEN. After a change of residence, the cards of the entire family should be sent out as soon as possible.

RESTAURANTS. If at a table, and a woman bows, the man should rise and bow in return. If a man is one of a party sitting at a table, and a woman with her escort stops to pass greetings, he should rise and stand until they depart.

One man introduced to another who is surrounded by male friends should rise to acknowledge the honor of the introduction.

When a man is with a woman he should exercise great care in recognizing male acquaintances who may be in doubtful company. He should avoid being in such company himself when in such places.

Smoking in restaurants is a general custom. The rules of the house govern this.

All fees to the waiters should be paid by the one who pays the bills. If a woman is paying her own bill when with a man, it is in order for her to fee the waiter.

RIBBONS AT CHURCH WEDDINGS. One way of distinguishing the pews reserved for the family, relatives, and dearest friends of both families is the placing of white ribbons at the dividing pews. Before the arrival of the bride, the ushers, in pairs, at the same time, untie these ribbons, and stretch them along the outside of these pews, and thus enclose the guests and bar further intrusion.

If these ribbons are used, it is a good plan to enclose in the wedding invitation a card giving number of pew.

The advantage of not using ribbons is the avoidance of any possible discrimination.

RICE AT WEDDINGS. The throwing of rice is to be discouraged; but if it is to be done, the maid of honor should prepare packages of rice and hand them to the guests, who throw it after the bridal couple as they leave the house for their wedding trip.

RIDING.

MEN. When riding with a woman, a man should always assist her both to mount and to alight, even if a groom is present.

It is customary for the woman to set the pace, and for the man, who always rides on her right, to accommodate himself to her-- trotting, galloping, or walking his horse as she may do.

He should always be ready to open all gates for her, and to do all things that will make the riding pleasant for her. If at a fox-hunt, this would mean that he must be ready to sacrifice much of his personal pleasure that she may enjoy herself.

DRESS. There is a perfectly well-accepted dress for men who ride in the park, though it is open to elderly men to wear clothes less pronounced.

The correct dress is full riding-breeches, close-fitting at the knee, leggings, a high-buttoned waistcoat, and a coat with the conventional short cutaway tails. The hat is an alpine or a derby, and the tie the regulation stock. These, with riding-gloves and a riding-crop, constitute the regular riding-dress for a young man.

A man should always consult his tailor, that the dress in all its details may be strictly up to date.

WOMEN--DRESS. There is a well-prescribed riding-dress for women as for men. The habit of dark material, with skirt falling just over the feet when in the saddle, and the close-fitting waist, with long or short tails, together with the white collar and black or white tie, constitute the regulation dress. The derby hat is smaller than formerly. Gloves of a dark color and a crop with a bone handle are always in place. Any jewelry, save that which is absolutely necessary, should be shunned.

In summer it is permissible to modify this costume.

As in the case of a man, a woman should consult a tailor of good practical experience, that her costume may be in the correct style.

RING, ENGAGEMENT. See ENGAGEMENT RING.

RING, WEDDING. See WEDDING RING.

RISING FROM THE TABLE. The signal to leave the table is always given by the women, and the men rise to let the women pass. At a formal dinner the signal is given by the hostess.

SALT is best taken up with the tip of the knife.

SALTED NUTS are eaten with the fingers.

SEAT OF HONOR is at the right of the host.

SECOND HELPING. At formal dinner parties, luncheons, and breakfasts, second helpings are never offered by the host or hostess, and should not be asked for by the guests. This is only permissible at a small dinner party or at the daily family meal.

Of course, this does not apply to a second glass of water, for which the guest asks, or for wine. It is the duty of the waiter to see that the guest is constantly supplied.

SECOND MARRIAGES. See WIDOWS--WEDDINGS.

SECRETARY OF AGRICULTURE. See AGRICULTURE, SECRETARY OF.

SECRETARY OF COMMERCE. See COMMRCE, SECRETARY OF.

SECRETARY OF INTERIOR. SEE INTERIOR, SECRETARY OF.

SECRETARY OF NAVY. SEE NAVY, SECRETARY OF.

SECRETARY OF STATE. See STATE, SECRETARY OF.

SECRETARY OF TREASURY. See TREASURY, SECRETARY OF.

SECRETARY OF WAR. SEE WAR, SECRETARY OF.

SEEDS should be removed from the mouth with the aid of a fork, or dropped into the half-closed hand.

SENATOR--HOW ADDRESSED. An official letter begins: Sir, and ends: I have, sir, the honor to remain your most obedient servant.

A social letter begins: My dear Senator Wilson, and ends: Believe me, most sincerely yours.

The address on the envelope is: Senator John J. Wilson, or, To the Hon. John J. Wilson.

SERVANTS-TIPPING. It is customary for guests leaving a house after a visit to tip the servants, unless positively requested by the hostess not to do so. The average tip would be one dollar, with more for extra attention.

SHAKING HANDS.

DANCES. It is not customary to shake hands at formal dances.

HOST AND HOSTESS. The host and the hostess should shake hands with each guest as they arrive.

If guest takes leave of host and hostess, they should shake hands. If they are sur- rounded by guests, a pleasant nod of farewell is admissible.

MEN. At a wedding, the opera, or a dance, and all very formal occasions, gloves should not be removed when shaking hands.

If the hostess wears gloves at any formal affair, a man wears his when he shakes hands with her. He should give a slight pressure only.

A man with hands gloved should never shake hands with a woman without an apology for so doing, unless she likewise wears gloves. A sudden meeting, etc., may make a handshaking in gloves unavoidable. Unless the other party is gloved, a man should apologize.

When men are introduced to men, they always shake hands. It is bad form to crush the hand when shaking it.

When introduced to a woman, men should bow, but not offer to shake hands.

CALLS. If the woman is seated when a man enters the room, she rises to greet him, and, if she wishes, shakes hands. She has the option to shake hands or not, and should make the first advances. It is bad form for him to do so.

WOMEN. Upon introduction, a woman may shake hands with either men or women, but a slight inclination of the body, a pleasant smile, and an appropriate remark are more correct.

A young girl, upon being introduced to an older woman, should await the action of the elder, who will shake hands if kindly disposed.

If one person extends the hand, it should be accepted without the slightest hesitation, to avoid embarrassment.

SIGNING LETTERS. See ADDRESSING AND SIGNING LETTERS.

SILK WEDDINGS. This is the name of the forty-fifth wedding anniversary, and is now seldom observed. If it is, any article of silk would be appropriate as a gift, and congratulations may be extended in accepting or declining the invitations. The invitations may have the words: No presents received. An entertainment usually follows.

SILVER WEDDINGS. After twenty-five years of married life, the silver wedding may be celebrated. On the invitations sent out may be engraved the words: No presents received.

Congratulations may be extended in accepting or declining the invitation. Any article of silver is appropriate as a gift. An entertainment follows.

At a silver wedding the invitations may be appropriately engraved in a silver-gray color, and the decorations are usually of the same color.

SLIPPERS-THROWING AT WEDDINGS. The throwing of slippers after the bridal couple on their leaving the house for their wedding trip is in poor taste.

SMOKING. At a dinner when the women rise, the men also rise and remain standing until the former leave the room, when cigars and coffee are served. Sometimes the men accompany the women to the drawing-room, bow, and then return to the dining-room for the coffee and cigars, where they remain about half an hour.

Smoking in restaurants is a general custom, but the rules of the house govern it. Theatres provide rooms for it, hence it should be limited to them.

There should be no smoking at afternoon entertainments, unless the men are requested to do so by the host and hostess.

At balls a room for smoking is generally provided. Smoking is not in good taste if a man is going to dance, as the odor of tobacco clings to the clothing. There should be no smoking in the dressing-rooms.

Smoking a pipe in the street is becoming more common. It is poor taste, however, on a fashionable street. At best, any smoking in the street is bad form.

Expectorating on the pavement is a most reprehensible habit. If it must be done, a man should step to the curb and expectorate in the street.

DANCES. Smoking should not be allowed in the dressing-room, but a special room should be provided. Men who dance should not smoke until leaving the house.

IN PRESENCE OF WOMEN. Smoking in the street while walking with a woman should never be indulged in, although she seemingly is agreeable to it. If a man is smoking, and he stops to speak to a woman, he should throw away his cigar or cigarette.

A man should not smoke in the presence of women unless bidden by them to do so. Few women care to say that it is disagreeable when asked, hence the better course is to await permission.

WOMEN. If a woman has true regard for herself, she should not indulge in smoking; if she does, it should be in absolute privacy.

SON.

BALLS. A son should do all in his power to make the ball a success by finding partners for the women having none, seeing that the men are introduced to the women, and taking in to supper a woman without an escort.

CARDS. When a mother is calling, she can leave cards of her son for the host and hostess if it is impossible for him to do so himself.

A son entering society can have his cards left by his mother for a host and hostess. Invitations to entertainments will follow.

SON (YOUNGER) OF DUKE-HOW ADDRESSED. An official letter begins: My Lord, and ends: I have the honor to remain your Lordship's obedient servant.

The address on the envelope is: To the Right Honorable the Lord John J. Kent.

A social letter begins: My dear Lord John J. Kent, and ends: Believe me, my dear Lord John, faithfully yours.

The address is: To the Lord John J. Kent.

SON (YOUNGER) OF EARL-HOW ADDRESSED, An official letter begins: Sir, and ends: I have the honor to remain your obedient servant.

A social letter begins: Dear Mr. Wilson, and ends: Believe me, dear Mr. Wilson, sincerely yours.

The address on the envelope is: To the Honorable John Wilson.

SON (YOUNGER) OF MARQUIS--HOW ADDRESSED. An official letter begins: My Lord, and ends: I have the honor to remain your Lordship's obedient servant.

The address on the envelope is: To the Right Honorable the Lord John J. Kent.

A social letter begins: My dear Lord John J. Kent, and ends: Believe me, my dear Lord Kent, faithfully yours.

The address is: To the Lord John J. Kent,

SON (YOUNGER) OF VISCOUNT-HOW ADDRESSED. An official letter begins: Sir, and ends: I have the honor to remain your obedient servant.

A social letter begins: Dear Mr. Wilson, and ends: Believe me, dear Mr. Wilson, sincerely yours.

The address on the envelope is: To the Honorable John Wilson.

SOUP should be taken from the side of the spoon without noise and without the plate being tipped. Men with mustaches are privileged in this respect, and may take the soup from the end of the spoon.

SOUVENIRS.

BRIDESMAIDS. These are given by the bride to her bridesmaids a few days before the wedding, and take the form of fans or jewelry of some kind that may be worn at the wedding.

A good time to present them is when the bride gives a farewell dinner or luncheon to her bridesmaids.

Failing this, they may be sent a few days before the wedding.

The souvenirs should, of course, be all the same in value and in style.

USHERS. The souvenirs given by the groom to the ushers usually take the form of scarf-pins or cuff-buttons. Sometimes the groom also gives the ushers neckties and gloves.

A good time for their distribution is at the farewell bachelor dinner.

SPONSORS. Only relatives and near friends should be asked to act as sponsors at a christening. Two women and one man are asked as sponsors for a girl, and one woman and two men for a boy, though one man and one woman are sufficient in either case.

These may be invited by note or personal call to act as sponsors, and should answer by note or personal call.

A few days before the ceremony the sponsor should send a christening gift addressed to the child, and the giver's card, with a suitable sentiment written on it, should be sent with the gift.

A man may give some article of silver, and, if a wealthy relative, a bank-book for money deposited in the child's name.

A woman may present the child with a garment, a carriage, a cradle, or some similar article.

It is in good taste for the sponsors to call immediately on the parents, to send flowers to the mother, and to show that they are pleased with the compliment.

The godfather at the ceremony assents to the vows, and later, at the drinking of the wine, should propose both the health of the child and that of its mother.

SPOON. The spoon should never be in the cup while drinking, but should be left in the saucer. It is used in eating grapefruit, fruit salads, small and large fruit (when served with cream), puddings, jellies, porridges, preserves, and boiled eggs.

SR, The letters SR. (abbreviation for Senior) are sometimes added to a woman's name on her card when her son has the same name as his father, and it is necessary to distinguish between the cards of the daughter-in-law and the mother-in-law.

If both become widows, and yet wish to retain their husbands' Christian names, the daughter-in-law would add Jr. on her cards.

STAG PARTIES. A party composed of men exclusively is sometimes so designated. They are usually informal in character, but may be as elaborate in detail as desired.

DRESS. The Tuxedo coat and black tie is worn, unless at a formal stag party, when evening dress is appropriate.

STATE, SECRETARY OF-HOW ADDRESSED. An official letter begins: Sir, and ends: I have, sir, the honor to remain your most obedient servant.

A social letter begins: My dear Mr. Wilson, and ends: I have the honor to remain most sincerely yours.

The address on the envelope is: Hon. John J. Wilson, Secretary of State.

STATIONERY.

MEN. The variations from plainness and quietness in the use of stationery that are permitted women are denied to men. Their paper is never perfumed, and all fancy styles are in poor taste.

For his social correspondence a man should use white or gray linen or bank-note unruled paper, folding once in the envelope.

He may, of course, use for social correspondence his club stationery.

Under no circumstances should he use his business stationery for social correspondence.

WOMEN. Unruled plain white or gray paper, that folds once in the envelope, and black ink, are the standard materials for social correspondence.

While it is permissible to use some of the latest fancy stationery, care should be taken that it is quiet in taste, and that all merely temporary variations are avoided.

While it is better not to use perfumed paper, if any perfume is used it should be extremely delicate.

Elderly women are apt to favor Irish linen or similar stationery.

STRANGERS-INVITATIONS TO A BALL ASKED FOR BY FRIENDS. See BALLS-INVITATIONS ASKED FOR STRANGERS.

STREET-CARS AND OTHER CONVEYANCES.

MEN. The old custom of a man giving up his seat in a street-car to a woman is being gradually done away with. This is due largely to the fact that women are now so extensively engaged in commercial business that they are constant riders at the busy hours, end thus come into direct competition with men.

A well-bred man, however, will show his manliness by giving any woman his seat and standing himself, as she is less fitted for such hardships and annoyances. A man should always give his seat to an elderly woman, one accompanied with children, or one apparently weak and sickly. In giving his seat to a woman, a man should politely bow and raise his hat.

It is good form for a man to assist a woman getting on or off a car. If a man is accompanied by a woman when she leaves the car, he should help her off the car.

A man should always be polite and courteous toward a conductor, as the latter's position is a hard and trying one.

A man should never cross his legs or keep his feet extended in the passageway.

If a man finds it necessary to crowd into a car already full, he should do so with consideration and politeness, and with an apology for pressing against any one. It is better to stand than to crowd yourself into a small space between those who are seated.

EXPENSES. A man traveling with another man can pay the latter's fare if he wishes. But if he is accompanied by a woman he should pay her fare. If he is in the car, and other acquaintances, men or women, enter, they should pay their own fares.

WOMEN. A woman should not look with a pained and injured air at the men passengers because no one of them has offered her a seat. The great influx of women into the commercial world, and their being thrown into direct competition with men, has largely done away with the fine old custom of men giving up their seats to women. The impoliteness of many women in accepting a seat as a matter of right and not of courtesy, and perhaps without a "Thank you," has helped largely to bring about the present state of affairs. No woman of ordinary good manners should fail to express her thanks for the courtesy proffered. If a woman is offered a seat she should accept it at once-without urging.

A man may assist a woman in getting off a car. If a woman is accompanied by a man and she leaves the car, he should assist her to alight.

A woman should wait till a car absolutely stops before she gets on or off, and she should face the front when leaving the car.

If possible, a woman should have her car-fare handy or easy of access-preferably in her hand-before entering the car if it is crowded. A woman should avoid crowding into a small space between others, and it is better for her to stand than to occupy barely the edge of a seat. If it is absolutely necessary for her to enter a crowded car, she should do so with an apology to those whom she may crowd.

CONDUCTOR. A conductor occupies a difficult and trying position, and will always appreciate any courtesy shown him by a woman. If a woman desires a transfer, she should let him know in ample time; if she wants any information from him, she should ask him when paying her fare, and should indicate her desire to leave the car at least a block ahead of her street. A woman should not trust to a conductor to remember her street, even if she has asked him, but should look out for the street herself.

EXPENSES. If a woman is in a car and a man joins her, and the fare is not yet collected, she should pay her own fare. But if she is traveling with an escort she should not offer to pay her fare, as her escort pays the expenses.

STREET ETIQUETTE.

MEN. If a man is passed on the street without any recognition by an acquaintance, he should hesitate before accepting it as a direct cut, as it may have been an oversight. If it is repeated, he will know its full meaning.

To pass a person whom one knows and to look straight at him without recognition is the rudest way of dropping an acquaintance.

A man should avoid loud and boisterous behavior.

If a man is compelled to force his way through a crowded street, he should do so courteously and with an apology to any one inconvenienced by his act.

In walking three or four abreast, men should be careful not to obstruct the thoroughfare, but should quickly fall into single file when necessary.

A man should greet his acquaintances on the street quietly and courteously, and if on a crowded street, should step out of the way of persons and be brief in his remarks.

In all public places and conveyances a man should offer his seat to a woman, though he is not expected to do so when reserved seats can be obtained--as, in a theatre, at an opera, etc.

ACCIDENTS. In case of accident or danger a man should protect the woman whom he escorts, and take her to a place of safety. If her clothing is torn, or she has met with some accident of which she is unaware, a man may, if he desires, politely raise his hat and call her attention to the fact. If by accident a man jostles a woman or steps upon her dress, he should raise his hat, bow, and apologize, whether he knows her or not.

BOWING. A man should not bow to a woman until she has first recognized him, unless they are old acquaintances.

A man should acknowledge the salutation of a woman on the street, even if he does not know her, as it saves her from embarrassment at her mistake.

When bidding farewell to a woman after a conversation on the street, a man should bow and raise his hat.

If a man offers his seat to a woman in a car or other conveyance, he should raise his hat and bow, while her escort acknowledges the courtesy by doing the same.

When a man opens a door for a woman unknown to him, he should bow, while she enters in advance of him.

A man should raise his hat and bow on all occasions when offering any courtesy to a woman, whether stranger or acquaintance.

A man may bow to an elderly man or person of official position.

A man may offer his services to a woman in crossing a crowded thoroughfare, and should raise his hat and bow when she is safely over, but should, make no comment unless she does so first. He may also offer her assistance in getting on or off a car, raising his hat and bowing without remark.

If a man is accompanied by a woman and another man extends a courtesy to her, he should acknowledge it by bowing and giving a polite "Thank you."

If when walking with a man a woman meets a male acquaintance who bows, her escort should raise his hat and bow, though the two men are strangers to each other. If the escort meets a man known to him, both men should raise their hats and bow.

CANES AND UMBRELLAS. These should be carried vertically, never horizontally, thereby endangering other persons' eyes. Especially is this important when entering cars or going up long flights of steps-as, the stairs of the elevated railroad.

CONVERSATION. A man who meets a woman, and desires to engage in conversation with her, should ask permission to accompany her. If this is granted, he may proceed a short distance, unless requested to go farther.

When meeting a woman on the street and stopping to converse with her, a man should raise his hat and replace it, as it is not now in good form for a man to remain bareheaded until requested by the woman to replace his hat.

A man should avoid stopping a woman on the street to engage her in conversation.

Only an intimate acquaintance with a woman warrants a man joining her on the street. If it is not agreeable, it may be very embarrassing to her.

SMOKING. A man should never smoke while walking with a woman on a street. Smoking on fashionable thoroughfares is bad form.

A man should avoid expectorating upon a sidewalk, and, if it must be done, should walk to the curb and use the street for that purpose.

WALKING. A man should not walk between two women, but at the side nearest the curb.

When walking with a woman, a man should walk near the curb, unless passing an obstruction-as, a building in course of construction-when she should have the outer side to protect her from harm, or from coming in contact with disagreeable things.

A man should offer his right arm to a woman, but this is rarely necessary in the daytime. It is essential, however, and proper for him to do so after dark.

WOMEN. Conduct on the street should always be reserved. It is bad form to loudly laugh or to boldly glance at the passers-by, especially men.

Women should never walk three or four abreast.

Women may salute each other with a bow and a handshake, but a kiss in public is no longer in good form.

During a promenade, where friends pass and repass, it is not necessary to exchange greetings to each other.

A polite "Thank you," with a bow and a smile, should be the reward of any man extending a courtesy to a woman.

BOWING. It is the woman's privilege to determine whom she will publicly recognize, and therefore she should bow first to all men whom she desires to favor. This formality is, however, unnecessary with intimate friends.

UMBRELLAS. These should be carried vertically, and never horizontally under the arm.

WALKING. If a woman is walking with a man, and another man stops to speak, it would be in exceeding bad taste to ask him to join her.

A woman should take a man's right arm, but only after dark, unless for some special reason-as, weakness, etc.-it is necessary.

If a woman is walking alone, and a man of her acquaintance stops and speaks, he may ask permission to accompany her farther, which, if agreeable, should be granted. She may stop for a few moments' chat, and shake hands if she wishes. If he stands before her with uncovered head, she should promptly ask him to replace his hat. She should not block the thoroughfare, and should take the initiative if he does not step to one side. If agreeable, an invitation may be extended to him to walk a short distance.

SUBSCRIPTION BALLS. MEN. Shortly after receiving an invitation to a subscription ball, a man should leave a card for the patroness inviting him.

INVITATIONS. In addition to the regular invitations, it is customary to guard against the admission of persons not really invited by the use of vouchers to be shown at the hall door, or some similar precaution is taken.

When a subscriber sends an invitation and a voucher, he should send in the same envelope one of his calling cards.

SUNDAY CALLS. Informal calls may be made on Sunday after three o'clock by business and professional men, provided there are no religious or other scruples on the part of those receiving the calls.

Men should wear afternoon dress.

SUPPERS GIVEN BY MEN--WOMEN. A young woman may accept a man's invitation, provided she has the consent of her mother or guardian, and is assured that a chaperone will be present.

SUPPERS--MEN. Suppers are generally for men. The hours are from ten to eleven. A man can give such entertainments in bachelor apartments or restaurant, and if women are invited, chaperones should be present.

The invitations may be given personally, written, or a visiting-card may be used, giving hour and date. If the supper is given in honor of a special guest, engraved cards or note sheets are used.

Suppers may be of various kinds--such as Fish, Game, Wine, Champagne.

SUPPERS AND THEATRE PARTIES. MEN. A man should not invite a young woman to a theatre party or supper without inviting her mother or a chaperone to accompany them. At large theatre parties or suppers, when there are ten or more guests, several chaperones should be invited. Any married or elderly unmarried woman can act as chaperone, care being taken that they are well-known and agreeable to all, as much of the pleasure of the evening depends upon them. CARRIAGES. A conveyance holding a large party can be sent to take invited guests to the entertainment. The chaperone should be called for first, and should be the last one to be left at home upon returning. The chaperones may use their own carriages and call for guests if they desire. If the chaperones call for the guests, the men can be met at the place of amusement. Conveyances should be provided for guests.

SUPPERS GIVEN BY BACHELORS. See BACHELORS' SUPPERS.

TABLE ETIQUETTE. It is correct to take a little of all that is offered, though one may not care for it. Bend slightly over the plate when carrying the food to the mouth, resuming upright position afterward.

When drinking from a cup or glass, raise it gracefully to the mouth and sip the contents. Do not empty the vessel at one draught.

Guests should not amuse themselves by handling knife or fork, crumbling bread, or leaning their arms on the table. They should sit back in their chairs and assume an easy position.

A guest at a dinner should not pass a plate or any article to another guest, or serve the viands, unless asked to do so by the hostess.

Upon leaving the table, push the chair back far enough to be out of the way of others.

ACCIDENTS. Accidents, or anything that may be amiss at the table, should be unobserved by a guest unless he is the cause of it. In that event some pleasant remark as to his awkwardness should be made and no more. The waiter should attend to the matter at once.

If a fork or a spoon is dropped it should not be picked up by the guest, but another used, or ask the waiter to provide one.

CONVERSATION. Aim at bright and general conversation, avoiding all personalities and any subject that all cannot join in. This is largely determined by the character of the company. The guests should accommodate themselves to their surroundings.

See also FINGER-BOWL, KNIFE AND FORK, SECOND HELPING, SEEDS, SPOON, TOOTHPICKS, WINES, and names of individual fruits and foods--as, APPLES,

BREAD, etc.

TALKING--THEATRES. Conversation during the progress of the play or the opera should be avoided and confined to the intermissions. The theatregoer should avoid all noise, gestures, or actions that would annoy others.

A man would be justified, when annoyed by a person talking loud near him, in asking him politely to speak lower.

TEAS.

Invitations. These need no acknowledgment.

Given by bachelors. See BACHELORS' TEAS.

Afternoon. See AFTERNOON TEAS.

High. See HIGH TEA.

TELEPHONE INVITATIONS. Telephone invitations should be sent only to those with whom the utmost intimacy exists, and who will pardon the informality.

THEATRE. A young man may invite a young woman to the theatre or opera, even if he has but a slight acquaintance with her, but of course he should secure the permission of her parents or chaperone.

It is correct for the young man to inquire if the young woman prefers a box, or, if not, he should state in what part of the house he proposes to secure seats. This will enable her to determine how to dress.

If the young woman wears street toilette, her escort may take her in any public conveyance, but if she wears evening dress, he should provide a carriage.

At the theatre he should precede the woman down the aisle to the seat or box; but if it is the latter, he should open the door and wait for her to pass.

A man may use his judgment as to the aisle seat. If a better view can be had, or seemingly objectionable people are next the inside seat, it is perfectly proper to give the woman the aisle seat.

A man should never leave his companion between the acts. The custom of both men and women going into the foyer at that time is a growing one, and is a relief to the audience.

Refreshments at some fashionable place may follow after the entertainment.

For a man to call on an acquaintance in an opera box does not relieve one of the duty of making a formal call in return for social favors.

BONNET. A woman of any consideration will either wear no bonnet at all or remove it as soon as the curtain is raised.

It would be in place for a man or woman whose view is hampered by a bonnet to politely ask the wearer to remove it, and when it is done, to thank her.

MEN--LEAVING CARDS. After a theatre party given by a man, he should call within three days on the woman he escorted or leave his card.

PRECEDENCE. In entering a theatre a man precedes the women of his party, but after he has handed his coupons to the ushers he gives the women precedence, and follows them to their seats.

TALKING. Conversation during the progress of the play or the opera should be avoided, and confined to the intermissions.

The theatregoer should avoid all noise, gestures, or actions tending to annoy others or to render himself conspicuous.

A man would be justified, when annoyed by a person talking loud near him, in asking him politely to speak lower.

THEATRE AND OPERA PARTIES.

GIVEN BY MEN. A man giving a theatre or opera party should secure one or more chaperones if women are to be present.

CALLS. The host should call upon his guests within three days or a week after the event.

CARRIAGES. The host may, if he choose, send carriages or a stage to collect all the guests. This is a formal and agreeable way to begin the evening's pleasure. The chaperone should be called for first. A more informal way is quite popular. The invitations having been given and accepted, the host informs each of his guests as to the others, and leaves a ticket with each one. All then meet informally at the place of amusement. If a dinner is given before the entertainment, carriages are provided to convey the guests to the theatre.

CHAPERONE. A chaperone should always be present if women are to be members of the party. And if a stage or carriage calls for the guests, it should call first for the chaperone.

The chaperone who acts as hostess should decide the hour to close the festivities.

DINNERS. If a dinner is given before the performance, it is generally given at six o'clock, the usual customs being followed. If preferred, the dinner may follow the performance, and may be given at any fashionable restaurant or hotel. If it is given before the play, at its termination the guests are conveyed in carriages or stage to the theatre at the expense of the host.

After the entertainment it is a good plan for the party to return to the banqueting-room to partake of slight refreshments.

DRESS. Men wear evening dress. Women wear full evening dress.

INVITATIONS. He may invite his guests in person or by note. In either case he should secure the parents' permission to allow the young women to attend, and should be ready to supply all information regarding the men who will be present, and also the chaperones.

MEN. The escorts should see the women home unless they are called for by the male members of their families, in which case they may be accompanied to their conveyances. If a young woman is called for by her maid in a carriage, her escort may take her home.

Intimacy of the parties largely regulates the etiquette of such occasions. They can decide whether evening or street dress shall be worn, and seat themselves accordingly. A carriage should be provided.

When entering an opera or theatre box for a short call, a man should stand and bow, making some pleasant remark to the chaperone. If there is an empty chair, he may sit and talk a few minutes and retire as others enter.

WOMEN. Between the acts it is perfectly proper to go into the foyer with the escort, who should carry the woman's wraps and see that all her wants are attended to. Should she desire anything, she should call on him first.

The hat or bonnet should be removed.

In a box the women occupy the front row while the men sit or stand in the rear.

A woman should avoid conspicuous manners, loud conversation, laughing, or acting in any way to attract attention.

GIVEN BY WOMEN. This is a popular form of entertainment during the season. They are given by married women, and the guests are invited by note. A dinner is given at the house or at a restaurant before the departure for the opera or play. Refreshments may also be given after the entertainment at either the house or restaurant. At the dinner the same ceremonies are followed as to arrangements of guests and escorts as at any formal dinner.

TOASTS--WEDDINGS. Toasts to the bride and groom are customary at the wedding breakfast or supper.

If the groom gives a farewell bachelor dinner, he should propose a toast to the bride.

THEATRE PARTIES. See also CHAPERONE-MEN. CHAPERONE-THEATRE.

THIRD PERSON-USED IN CORRESPONDENCE. While it was formerly the correct usage to begin formal communications in the third person, it is now the custom to begin such letters: MY DEAR MRS SMITH, or MADAM.

The third person would be used only in writing to a workman, a strange servant, or a business firm.

TIN WEDDING. After ten years of marriage, occurs the tin wedding. The invitations sent out may have the words: NO PRESENTS RECEIVED. Congratulations may be extended in accepting or declining the invitation.

Every conceivable device made of tin is appropriate as a gift, but, as these are limited, ingenuity may be displayed in getting up oddities. An entertainment may follow.

TIPPING. At balls. It is not customary to tip the servants at a private ball, but at a public one it is usual to give a tip to the attendant at the cloak-room.

At christenings. The father usually gives the nurse at a christening a sum of money, and the mother gives her some article of dress or piece of jewelry.

At house; parties. See HOUSE PARTIES. GUESTS. TIPPING SERVANTS. Also under names of servants--as, COACHMAN.

TITLES. MEN'S CARDS. Men having titles use them before their names--as, REVEREND, REV. MR., REV. DR., Army and Navy titles, and officers on the retired list.

LL.D. and all professional titles are placed after the name. Political and judicial titles are always omitted.

Physicians may use DR. before or M.D. after their names. On cards intended for social use, office hours and other professional matters are omitted.

WOMEN'S CARDS. The same principles govern the titles on women's cards, with the addition that women should never use titles of their husbands.

TOOTHPICKS should not be used in public. If necessity requires it, raise the napkin over the mouth, with the hand behind it, using the toothpick as quickly as possible.

TOWN, RETURNING TO-WOMEN. Cards of the entire family should be sent by mail to all acquaintances when returning after a prolonged absence.

When using cards, if out of town, the place of a woman's permanent residence can be written on the card thus: NEW YORK. PHILADELPHIA.

TRAVELERS' VISITING-CARDS. A woman visiting a place for a length of time should mail to her friends a visiting-card containing her temporary address.

A man in a similar situation should call upon his friends, and if he does not find them at home should leave his card.

TRAVELING.

MEN WITH WOMEN. When traveling with a woman, a man should see to the checking and care of her baggage.

MEN. As it is exceedingly trying and difficult for a woman to stand in a railroad train while it is in motion, it is the height of good manners for a man to offer her his seat and to insist on her taking it.

EXPENSES. On a short boat or railroad trip a man should pay the expenses of a woman who accompanies him by his invitation. But on a long trip she should insist on paying her share, and he should accept her decision. Of course, he is at liberty, however, to pay all the expenses of slight entertainments-as, fruit, magazines, etc.

He should see to the care of her baggage and all other details.

PARLOR-CAR. When traveling a long distance accompanied by a woman, a man should secure seats in the parlor-car.

While it is admissible to offer assistance to a woman traveling in a parlor-car without an escort, it should be done in the most polite and delicate manner, and be perfectly agreeable to her.

WOMEN. If a woman arrives at a strange place, especially a large city, and no one meets her, she should ask the station porter to attend to her baggage and all such details, and, if traveling farther, to see to her ticket and to find for her the right train.

If at the end of her journey she gives him the address she desires to go to and her trunk checks, he should procure a carriage for her. This saves her much worry and annoyance and needless risk.

The same suggestions apply to steamboat travel.

EXPENSES. If a woman is asked by a man to take a short boat or railroad trip, he should pay her fare and all other expenses. But if on a long trip--as, a summer outing--and she is escorted by a man, she should insist on paying her own fare and all expenses, allowing him, however, to pay the expenses of slight entertainment--as, fruit, magazines, etc.

PARLOR-CAR. Her escort should attend to all details of traveling. If she is traveling alone, she should always ride in the parlor-car and have the porter attend to her wants. While it may be proper to accept in a parlor-car attentions from a man if he is accompanied by a woman, the greatest caution is required if he is alone; in fact, it is well to be on one's guard, when traveling alone, against the attentions of both men and women.

TREASURY, SECRETARY OF--HOW ADDRESSED. An official letter begins: Sir, and ends: I have, Sir, the honor to remain your most obedient servant

A social letter begins: My Dear MR. Wilson, and ends: I have the honor to remain most sincerely yours.

The address on the envelope is: Hon. John J. Wilson, Secretary Of Treasury.

TROUSSEAU, WEDDING. The bride exhibits the trousseau at a dinner given to the bridesmaids and maid of honor a few days before the wedding.

TURNING DOWN CORNER OF VISITING-CARDS. This should not be done.

TUXEDO. The Tuxedo coat and waistcoat are worn at all informal affairs when no women are present, such as small theatre parties (when not occupying a box), bowling and card parties, restaurants, and the like.

It may be worn on the street in the evening with a low hat. A black tie should always be worn, and never, under any circumstances, a white one. See also EVENING DRESS--MEN.

UMBRELLAS. MEN CALLING ON WOMEN. When making a formal or brief call, the umbrella should be left in the hall.

CARRYING. Umbrellas should be carried vertically, never horizontally, thereby endangering other persons' eyes. Especially is this important when entering cars or going up long flights of steps--as, at an elevated railroad station.

USHERS. A sufficient number of ushers should be provided for to allow of two for each aisle. A good plan is to have one selected as the master of ceremonies, and for him to go to the church on the wedding-day in ample time to personally see that all the details have been carried out. They should be present at all rehearsals.

The ushers are usually presented by the groom with some small trinket, such as a pin, as a souvenir of the occasion.

CALLS. The ushers should call upon the married couple as soon as the latter have returned from their wedding trip.

CHURCH. The ushers should arrive at the church before the guests.

Each usher should have a list of all the intended guests for whom special places are set aside, and should check off the names of the guests as they arrive. He should know the various guests and where to place them; but if he does not know them personally, he should consult his list.

The upper ends of the middle aisles of both sides are usually reserved for invited guests, and are distinguished from the rest of the church by having a white ribbon or a string of flowers stretched across the aisle. The immediate family and special guests occupy the front seats, the family and the guests of the bride taking the left side and those of the groom the right side of the aisle. Other guests should be given the best seats, according to their priority in arriving.

It is in bad taste for an usher to reserve seats for his own friends as against the first-comers.

In seating guests, the usher should give his left arm to a woman and escort her to her seat while her escort follows.

Before the arrival of the bridal party the ushers take the ribbons at either end, and, walking the length of the aisle, close it against intrusion. Upon the arrival of the bride they form in pairs in the vestibule and lead the procession, followed by the bridesmaids, also in pairs. When they approach the altar they separate, one-half to the right and one-half to the left. The bridesmaids do likewise, and stand in front of the ushers.

At the conclusion of the ceremony they follow last in the procession to the vestibule, where, after giving their best wishes to the bride and congratulations to the groom, they hasten as soon as possible to the bride's home to assist in introducing and meeting the guests at the reception or breakfast.

DRESS. At a morning or afternoon wedding they wear black frock coats.

At an evening wedding they wear full evening dress, also white kid gloves, which are not removed during the ceremony. Hats should be left in the vestibule.

FLOWERS. If the boutonniers are given by the bride, they should go to her house to receive them and to have her place them in the lapels of their coats;

or the boutonniers may be kept at the church in the care of the sexton.

GLOVES. For morning or an afternoon wedding the gloves are gray. At an evening wedding the gloves are white kid. The gloves are not removed during the ceremony.

JEWELRY. They wear the scarf-pins or cuff- buttons given to them by the groom.

NECKTIES. At a morning or afternoon wedding the neckties are usually of some delicate color. At an evening wedding the neckties are white, as is customary with evening dress.

WEDDING BREAKFAST. The ushers pair off with the bridesmaids, and are usually seated at a table assigned to them.

WEDDING RECEPTIONS. The ushers, should introduce the guests to the groom and bride, calling the latter "Mr. and Mrs. A.," beginning with the relatives and friends, and continuing with the others till all have been introduced. In introducing the guests, the usher should offer his arm to the woman, and if not knowing her, should ask her her name, while her escort follows and is introduced at the same time. The bride may request the usher to introduce the guests to the parents.

VALET.

TIPS. It is customary for a man leaving after a house party to give to the valet who has waited upon him at least one dollar and more, in proportion for added attention.

WITH MASTER ON VISIT. As a general rule, few American men take their valets with them when they visit. But when such is the case, the valet would wait upon his master, and should give as little care to the household as possible.

VEIL

MOURNING. See Widow-Mourning.

WEDDING. This should be white. While its length depends upon the wishes of the bride, the long veil is more in keeping with the traditions and customs of the ceremony.

Verbal Invitations. All invitations should be sent by mail, and verbal invitations avoided if possible; if one is given, it should be followed by one in writing.

VICE-PRESIDENT--HOW ADDRESSED. An official letter begins: Sir, and ends, I have, sir, the honor to remain your most obedient servant.

A social letter begins: My dear Mr. Wilson, and ends: I have the honor to remain most sincerely yours.

The address on the envelope is: The Vice- President, John J. Wilson.

VISCOUNT--HOW ADDRESSED. An official letter begins: My Lord, and ends: I have the honor to be your Lordship's obedient servant.

The address on the envelope is: The Right Honorable Viscount Wilson.

A social letter begins: Dear Lord Wilson, and ends: Believe me, my dear Lord Wilson, very sincerely yours.

The address on the envelope is: To the Viscount Wilson.

VISCOUNTESS--HOW ADDRESSED. An official letter begins: Madam, and ends: I have the honor to remain your Ladyship's most obedient servant.

The address on the envelope reads: To the Right Honorable, the Viscountess of Kent.

A social letter begins: Dear Lady Kent, and ends: Believe me, dear Lady Kent, sincerely yours.

The address on the envelope reads: To the Viscountess of Kent.

VISCOUNT.

DAUGHTER OF. See Daughter of Viscount.

WIFE OF YOUNGER SON. See Wife of Younger Son of Viscount.

YOUNGER SON OF. See Son (Younger) of Viscount.

Visiting-cards. See Cards, Visiting.

VISITORS TO TOWN--CARDS. Visitors to town should send cards to every one whom they desire to see, with the address written on the cards.

VOUCHERS. These are safeguards against the admission of uninvited guests at a subscription ball, and take the form of cards to be shown at the door.

When a person sends one of these vouchers and an invitation to a person, he should en- close one of his calling cards.

"WALLFLOWERS." This is the name commonly applied to young women at a ball who do not dance because of lack of partners. It should be the aim of the hostess, with the aid of her sons and daughters, to find partners for such young women.

WAR, SECRETARY OF--HOW ADDRESSED, An official letter begins: Sir, and ends: I have, sir, the honor to remain your most obedient servant.

A social letter begins: My dear Mr. Wilson, and ends: I have the honor to remain most sincerely yours.

The address on the envelope is: Hon. John J. Wilson, Secretary of War.

WEDDING.

BREAKFAST. See Wedding Reception or Breakfast.

CAKE. At the conclusion of the wedding break- fast the cake is placed before the bride, who first cuts a piece, and then it is passed to the others. More often it is put up in small white boxes and given to the guests, or the boxes containing the cake are placed on a table in the hallway, and the guests each take one on their departure.

DAY. The wedding-day is named by the bride, and her mother's approval is asked by the groom.

It is not customary for the bride to see the groom on the wedding-day till she meets him at the altar.

KISS. The kiss in the ceremony is being done away with, especially at church weddings. Only the bride's parents and her most intimate friends should kiss her, and for others to do so is no longer good form.

RECEPTIONS OR BREAKFASTS. The married couple, on arriving at the house of the bride, place themselves in a convenient location, and, assisted by the best man, maid of honor, and the parents of both parties, receive the invited guests. Congratulations are given to the groom and best wishes to the bride.

A reception is more often given than a breakfast, as it allows more invitations and more freedom, and the refreshments are placed on the tables, so that the guests help themselves or are served by the bridesmaids.

The guests wait upon the married couple.

At a breakfast, when the congratulations are over, the breakfast is announced, and the married couple lead the way to the table reserved for them. Parents of both parties, the best man, and the maid of honor are usually placed at this table.

Guests leave a card for the host and hostess and another for the married couple.

Invitations are sent with the wedding invitations, but only to the nearest relatives and friends.

They should be immediately acknowledged, either by letter of acceptance or declination with regret.

TRIP. All details should be arranged before- hand by the best man, who knows the destination, and should keep it an inviolate secret, revealing it only in case of accident.

It is becoming the fashion for the married couple to do away with the trip, and instead to begin their married life in their own home.

VEIL. This should be white. While its length depends upon the wishes of the bride, the long veil is more in keeping with the traditions and customs of the wedding ceremony.

WOMEN-CARDS. When invitations have been received to the church but not to the wedding reception, cards should be sent to the bride's parents and to the bridal couple.

WEDDINGS.

AISLE PROCESSION. See Weddings-Procession Up the Aisle.

ANNIVERSARIES. See Anniversaries-Wedding.

ANNOUNCEMENTS. Announcement cards are sent the day after the wedding, and need not be acknowledged. They should be prepared beforehand and ready to be mailed. The expense is borne by the family of the bride. At a home or a private wedding, announcement cards can be sent to friends out of town.

AT HOME. See Home Weddings.

BEST MAN. See Best Man.

BEST WISHES. Best wishes should be given to the bride and congratulations to the groom.

BOUQUETS. The bouquet carried by the bride is furnished by the groom, who may also provide bouquets for the bridesmaids if he wishes.

BRIDE. See Bride.

BRIDESMAIDS. See Bridesmaids.

CAKE. See Wedding Cake.

CALLS. See Weddings-Invitations-Calls.

CARDS OF ADMISSION TO CHURCH. These cards are used at all public weddings held in churches, and when used no one should be admitted to the church without one. They are sent with the wedding invitations.

They are kept in stock by the stationer, and are not expensive.

CARDS, VISITING, AFTER MARRIAGE. Mr. and Mrs. cards are used by the wife only within one year after the marriage, after which separate cards are in order. These Mr. and Mrs. cards are used in sending gifts, congratulations, condolence, and at ceremonious affairs, when both the husband and wife are represented.

CARRIAGES. Carriages should be provided to take the bride and her family to the church and back to the house, and also the guests from the church to the receptions.

The expense is borne by the family of the bride, save for the carriage used by the groom, which takes him and the best man to the church, and later takes the married couple to the house, and after the reception, to the station.

CHOIR-BOYS. See CHOIR-BOYS AT WEDDINGS.

CONGRATULATIONS. Congratulations may be sent with letter of acceptance or declination of an invitation to a wedding to those sending the invitations. And if acquaintance with bride and groom warrant, a note of congratulations may be sent to them also.

Guests in personal conversation with the latter give best wishes to the bride and congratulations to the groom.

CHURCH. See BEST MAN--CHURCH. BRIDE--CHURCH. BRIDESMAIDS--CHURCH. GROOM--CHURCH. USHERS-CHURCH.

DANCES. It is not usual to have dances after the wedding.

DEPARTURE OF MARRIED COUPLE. See WEDDINGS--MARRIED COUPLE.

DRESS. See BEST MAN--DRESS. BRIDE--DRESS. GROOM-DRESS. WEDDINGS-GUESTS-DRESS, ETC.

EXPENSES. All the expenses are borne by the bride's family, except the fees for the license, clergyman, organist, and sexton. The wedding-ring, the carriages for the groom, ushers, best man, and the carriage which takes away the married couple, are also paid for by the groom.

He also furnishes souvenirs to the maid of honor and bridesmaids, best man and ushers, and all expenses of the wedding trip.

If the groom gives a farewell bachelor dinner, he bears all expenses.

FAREWELL BACHELOR DINNERS. See Groom- Farewell Dinner.

FAREWELL BRIDAL LUNCHEON. See Bride-- Farewell Luncheons.

FEES. The wedding fee, preferably gold or clean bills in sealed envelope, is given by the best man to the officiating clergyman. Custom leaves the amount to the groom, who should give at least five dollars or more, in proportion to his income and social position. The clergyman usually gives the fee to his wife.

FLOWER GIRLS. See Flower Girls.

FLOWERS are in general use. The quantity and quality of floral decorations must depend upon the taste and the wealth of the parties concerned.

BRIDE. The bride, if she desires, carries at the wedding ceremony a bouquet given by the groom. Flowers are sometimes dispensed with, and a Prayer-Book used.

CHURCH. In addition to the palms in the chancel, a string of flowers or white ribbons is stretched across the middle aisle, to reserve this place for the immediate family and specially invited guests.

USHERS. Boutonnieres, provided by the bride's family, should be given to the sexton by the florist on the wedding-day. They may be made of lilies of the valley, white roses, or the like.

Sometimes the ushers call at the house of the bride to have her fix them in the lapel of their coats.

GIFTS. The nearest members of each family should arrange among themselves what gifts to send, and thus avoid duplicates. Expensive presents are sent only by most intimate friends, and articles of utility by relatives or near friends. All gifts should be sent within two months of date of marriage, and should have thereon the woman's maiden name, initial cipher, or monogram, and should be acknowledged by the bride at the earliest moment, and not later than ten days after her marriage.

It is not in good taste to make an ostentatious display of the gifts, and if they are exhibited, the cards of the donors should be removed, and only intimate friends invited.

Those sending gifts should have the courtesy of an invitation to the wedding breakfast or reception.

If any gifts are sent to the groom, they should bear his initial.

A wedding invitation does not necessarily imply that a gift must be sent, as the sending of a gift is optional.

GROOM. See Groom.

GUESTS-BREAKFASTS OR RECEPTIONS. The invited guests leave the church for the bride's residence, and there are introduced by the ushers to the married couple and those standing up with them. If the guests are unknown to the ushers, they should give their names to one of them, who offers his left arm to the woman, while her escort follows and is introduced at the same time.

At the breakfast, guests are usually assigned places, but, if not, may take any seat. Only the specially invited guests await the departure of the married couple, which ends the reception or breakfast.

If boxes of wedding-cake are placed on a table, each guest takes one on his departure.

GUESTS-CALLS. Invited guests should call at least within ten days and leave their cards.

DRESS. Broadly speaking, at a morning or afternoon wedding the guest wears afternoon dress, and at an evening wedding evening dress. From the latter rule there are no deviations possible, but in the former there is greater latitude. Thus it would be possible for a man to wear a black cutaway coat at an afternoon wedding.

MEN. If the wraps are not left in the carriage, they are removed in the vestibule and are carried on the arm into the pew. A man follows the woman, who is escorted to the pew by the usher. At the end of the ceremony the guests should not leave until the immediate family have passed out.

Guests who are not invited to the breakfast or reception should not take offense, as the number present on such occasions is necessarily limited. These guests may seat themselves or are seated by the ushers, but not in the pews reserved for the family and specially invited guests.

WOMEN. No one should be present at a wedding in mourning, and it should be laid aside temporarily even by the mother, who wears purple velvet or silk. Women on entering the church take the usher's left arm, and are escorted to the pew, while their escort follows behind.

If they are immediate members of the family or are specially invited guests, they should give their names to the usher that he may seat them in the places reserved for them.

HATS OF GROOM AND OF BEST MAN. To do away with the possibility of the best man having to take care of the hats of groom and best man during the wedding ceremony, it is a good plan for both groom and best man to leave them in the vestry, and to have them carried out to the front of the church, ready for them at the end of the ceremony.

HOME See Home Weddings.

HOST. See Father of Bride.

HOSTESS. See Mother of Bride.

HOURS. Any hour from nine in the morning to nine in the evening is appropriate.

The morning hours are usually selected for quiet home affairs; twelve o'clock, or high noon, is still considered as the fashionable hour, while from three to six is the hour most convenient for all concerned.

Evening weddings are not very convenient, chiefly because it is not as easy to handle the details as in the daytime.

INVITATIONS. The woman's parents, guardians, or others give the wedding, send out the invitations, and bear all the expense of engraving and sending out the same. They are issued in the name of the one giving the wedding, and should be sent to near-by friends about twenty days in advance of the weddingday and earlier to out-of-town friends. With them are sent the invitation to the wedding breakfast or reception, and also the card of admission to the church.

The groom should supply a list of names of such persons as he desires to have present, designating his preference for those to be present at the breakfast or reception.

In addressing wedding invitations, two envelopes are used. The inner one, unsealed, bears the name only of the person addressed, and is enclosed in another envelope, sealed, bearing the address of the person invited.

Parents should, of course, order these invitations of a fashionable dealer in stationery, that good taste may be observed.

If the invitation contains an invitation to the breakfast or reception, it should be accepted or declined at once, and the answer sent to those issuing the invitation. If the invitation does not include a breakfast or reception invitation, no acknowledgment is necessary.

Should the wedding, however, be at home, and the guests limited in number, an acknowledgment should be sent.

If the invitations bear the letters R. S. V. P. an acknowledgment is necessary.

BRIDESMAIDS. At a large church wedding several invitations are usually given to the bridesmaids for their own personal use.

CALLS. Very intimate friends can call personally. Friends of the groom who have no acquaintance with the bride's family should send their cards to those inviting them.

Those who do not receive with wedding invitations and announcements At Home cards should not call, but consider themselves dropped from the circle of acquaintances of the married couple.

CARDS, LEAVING. If a person is invited to a wedding at a church, but not to the reception or breakfast, a card should be left or mailed both to the bride's parents and to the married couple.

Those present at the ceremony should leave cards in person for those inviting them, and if this is not possible, they can send them by mail or messenger.

Those invited but not present should send cards to those who invited them.

RECALLED. When for some good reason a wedding has to be canceled or postponed, the parents of the bride should, as soon as possible, send printed notices, giving the reasons, to all the invited guests.

JOURNEY. See Wedding Trip.

MAID OF HONOR. See Maid of Honor.

MARKING GIFTS. See Marking Wedding Gifts.

MARRIED COUPLE. Immediately after the wedding breakfast or reception, the bride, with her maid of honor, retires to change her clothes for those suitable for travel. The groom, with his best man, does likewise, and waits for his wife at the foot of the stairs.

As she comes down the stairs she lets fall her bridal bouquet among the bridesmaids, who strive to secure it, as its possession is deemed a lucky sign of being the next bride.

As the couple pass out of the front door it is customary for the guests to throw after them, for luck, rice, rose leaves, flowers, old shoes, etc.

The form to be used in signing the hotel register is: Mr. and Mrs. John K. Wilson. Good taste and a desire for personal comfort demand that their public acts and words be not of such a character as to attract attention.

See also Wedding Trip.

AT HOME. At the end of the wedding trip they proceed to their own home, and immediately send out their At Home cards, unless they have followed the better plan of enclosing them with their wedding cards.

They are at perfect liberty to send them to whom they please, and thus to select their friends. At these "At Homes" light refreshment is served, and the married couple wear full evening dress.

They are generally given a dinner by the bridesmaids, and are entertained by both families in appropriate ways.

MEN-DRESS. At a morning or afternoon wedding the groom, best man, and ushers wear afternoon dress, but at an evening wedding they wear evening dress.

For further details see Best Man--Dress. Groom--Dress. Ushers--Dress.

MOURNING should not be worn at a wedding, but should be laid aside temporarily, the wearer appearing in purple.

MUSIC. The organist and the music are usually selected by the bride. Before the arrival of the bride the organist plays some bright selection, but on her entering the church and passing up the aisle he plays the Wedding March.

PAGES. See Pages.

PRIVATE. See Private Wedding.

PROCESSION UP THE AISLE. Many styles are adopted for the procession up the aisle. A good order is for the ushers to come first in pairs, then the bridesmaids, maid of honor, and last the bride on her father's arm. At the altar the ushers and bridesmaids open ranks to allow the bride to pass through.

This order is usually reversed in the procession down the aisle.

RECALLING INVITATIONS. See Wedding Invitations (Recalled).

RECEPTIONS. See Wedding Receptions.

REHEARSALS. Rehearsals should be held even for a quiet home wedding, and at a sufficiently early date to insure the presence of all who are to participate.

REPORTERS. See Reporters--Weddings.

RIBBONS. See Ribbons at Church Weddings.

RICE. See Weddings--Throwing of Rice.

RING. This may be dispensed with, save in the Roman Catholic and in the Episcopal Church service. It is usually of plain gold, with initials of bride and groom and date of marriage engraved therein.

It is bought by the groom, who should give it to the best man to be kept till it is called for by the clergyman during the ceremony. It is worn on the third finger of the bride's left hand.

SECOND MARRIAGES. See Widows--Weddings.

SIGNING THE REGISTER. This is sometimes done by the bride and the groom, and takes place in the vestry, where the best man signs as chief witness and some of the guests as witnesses.

SOUVENIRS. See Souvenirs.

THROWING OF RICE. The throwing of rice is to be discouraged, but if it is to be done, the maid of honor should prepare packages of rice and hand them to the guests, who throw it after the bridal couple as they leave the house for their wedding trip.

TOASTS. Toasts to the bride and groom are customary at the wedding breakfast.

If the groom gives a farewell bachelor dinner, he should propose a toast to the bride.

TROUSSEAU. See Trousseau.

USHERS. See USHERS

WHITE RIBBONS. See RIBBONS.

WIDOWS. See WIDOWS--WEDDINGS.

WOMEN--DRESS. Women wear afternoon or evening dress, as the occasion requires. See also WIDOWS. GUESTS. WEDDINGS--GUESTS. WEDDINGS--WIDOWS.

WHITE RIBBONS AT WEDDINGS. See RIBBONS.

WIDOWS. CARD. During the first year of mourning a widow has no cards, as she makes no formal visits. After the first year, cards with border of any desired depth are used.

Either the husband's name or the widow's baptismal name may be used, but if in the immediate family the husband's name is duplicated, she should use her own name to avoid confusion. When her married son has his father's full name, the widow should add SR. to hers, as the son's wife is entitled to the name.

MOURNING. A widow should wear crape with a bonnet having a small border of white. The veil should be long and worn over the face for three months, after which a shorter veil may be worn for a year, and then the face may be exposed. Six months later white and lilac may be used, and colors resumed after two years.

STATIONERY, MOURNING. A widow's stationery should be heavily bordered, and is continued as long as she is in deep mourning. This is gradually decreased, in accordance with her change of mourning.

All embossing or stamping should be done in black.

WEDDINGS. Widows should avoid anything distinctively white, even in flowers--especially white orange blossoms and white veil, these two being distinctively indicative of the first wedding. If she wishes, she can have bridesmaids and ushers. Her wedding-cards should show her maiden name as part of her full name.

WIDOWERS--STATIONERY, MOURNING. The width of black on his stationery should be reduced as the interval is diminished.

All stamping should be in black.

WIFE--CARDS. Only the wife of the oldest member of the oldest branch may use her husband's name without the initials.

WIFE AND HUSBAND--CARDS, VISITING. When the wife is calling, she can leave cards of the husband and sons if it is impossible for them to do so themselves.

After an entertainment cards of the family can be left for the host and hostess by either the wife or any of the daughters.

WIFE OF BARONET--HOW ADDRESSED. An official letter begins: Madam, and ends: I have the honor to remain your Ladyship's most obedient servant.

A social letter begins: Dear Lady Wilson, and ends: Believe me, Lady Wilson, sincerely yours,

The address on the envelope is: To Lady Wilson.

WIFE OF A KNIGHT--HOW ADDRESSED. An official letter begins: Madam, and ends: I have the honor to remain your Ladyship's most obedient servant.

A social letter begins: Dear Lady Wilson, and ends: Believe me, Lady Wilson, sincerely yours.

The address on the envelope reads: To Lady Wilson.

WIFE OF YOUNGER SON OF BARON--HOW ADDRESSED. An official letter begins: Madam, and ends: I have the honor to remain, madam, your obedient servant.

A social letter begins: Dear Mrs. Wilson, and ends: Sincerely yours.

The address on the envelope is: To the Honorable Mrs. Wilson.

WIFE OF YOUNGER SON OF DUKE--HOW ADDRESSED. An official letter begins: Madam, and ends: I have the honor to remain, your Ladyship's most obedient servant.

The address on the envelope is: To the Right Honorable the Lady John Kent.

A social letter begins: Dear Lady John Kent, and ends: Believe me, dear Lady John Kent, faithfully yours.

The address is: To the Lady John Kent.

WIFE OF YOUNGER SON OF EARL--HOW ADDRESSED. An official letter begins:

Madam, and ends: I have the honor to remain, madam, your obedient servant.

A social letter begins: Dear Mrs. Wilson, and ends: Believe me, Mrs. Wilson, sincerely yours.

The address on the envelope is: To the Honorable Mrs. Wilson.

WIFE Of YOUNGER SON OF MARQUIS--HOW ADDRESSED. An official letter begins: Madam, and ends: I have the honor to remain your Ladyship's most obedient servant.

The address on the envelope is: To the Right Honorable, The Lady John Kent.

A social letter begins: Dear Lady John Kent, and ends: Believe me, dear Lady John Kent, faithfully yours.

The address is: To the Lady John Kent.

WIFE OF YOUNGER SON OF VISCOUNT--HOW ADDRESSED. An official letter begins: Madam, and ends: I have the honour to remain, madam, your obedient servant.

A social letter begins: Dear Mrs. Wilson, and ends: Sincerely yours.

The address on the envelope is: To the Honorable Mrs. Wilson.

WINE. A guest not caring for wine should turn down his glass and leave it in that position, or a mere sign of dissent when it is offered is sufficient.

WITNESSES AT WEDDINGS. If witnesses are needed, the best man selects them, and himself signs as the chief witness.

WOODEN WEDDINGS. Five years after the marriage comes the wooden wedding. On the invitations sent out may be engraved, if desired, No presents received. Congratulations may be extended in accepting or declining these invitations.

Those invited make suitable presents, and on this occasion any device made of wood is appropriate, including articles of utility--as, kitchen utensils, household ornaments, etc.

An entertainment usually follows,

WOOLEN WEDDINGS. This is the name of the fortieth wedding anniversary, and is seldom celebrated. The invitations may have the words: No presents received, and in accepting or declining the invitations, congratulations may be sent.

An entertainment should be provided, and any article of woolen would be appropriate as a gift.

WOMEN. BACHELOR'S DINNERS. Women do not call upon a bachelor after attending a dinner given by him.

CONDUCT TOWARD MEN. Male acquaintances should be carefully chosen, and great care exercised in accepting invitations from them.

When declining invitations from a man personally given, explanations are not necessary. If they are deemed desirable, they should be given as delicately as possible and without giving offence.

It is well never to receive men alone, unless they are most intimate friends. Compromising positions are easily fallen into, and a woman should be constantly on her guard.

WOMEN SERVANTS--TIPS. It is customary for guests at the end of a house-party visit to give tips to the maid for extra attention and taking care of the room, and also to the cook. The latter is usually tipped by the married men and bachelors.

AFTERNOON DRESS. See AFTERNOON DRESS--WOMEN.

AFTERNOON TEAS. See AFTERNOON TEAS (FORMAL) --WOMEN. AFTERNOON TEAS (INFORMAL)--WOMEN.

BACHELORS' DINNERS. See BACHELORS' DINNERS--WOMEN.

BACHELORS' TEAS. See BACHELORS' TEAS--WOMEN.

BALLS. See BALLS--WOMEN.

BOWING. See BOWING--WOMEN.

BREAKFASTS. See BREAKFASTS--WOMEN.

CALLS. See CALLS--WOMEN.

CARDS. See CARDS (VISITING)--WOMEN.

CHAPERONE. See CHAPERONE.

CHRISTENINGS. See CHRISTENINGS--WOMEN.

CONCLUSION OF LETTERS. See Conclusion of a Letter--Women.

COTILLIONS BY SUBSCRIPTIONS. See Cotillions by Subscriptions--Women.

DANCES. See Dances--Women.

DANCING. See Dancing--Women.

NEW ACQUAINTANCE. See New Acquaintances-- Women.

NEWCOMERS. See Newcomers--Residents' Duty to Women.

RIDING. See Riding--Women.

SALUTATIONS. See Salutations--Women.

SHAKING HANDS. See Shaking Hands--Women.

STATIONERY. See Stationery--Women.

STREET-CARS. See Street-cars--Women.

STREET ETIQUETTE. See Street Etiquette-- Women.

THEATRE PARTIES. See Theatre Parties-- Women.

TITLES. See Titles--Women.

TRAVELING. See Traveling--Women.

WEDDINGS. See Weddings--Women.

WRITTEN CARDS are in bad taste, but in case of necessity may be used. The name should be written in full if not too long, and should be the autograph of the sender.

YOUNGER SON. See Son (Younger).